Sustainable Food Systems

Sustainable Food Systems

The Role of the City

Robert Biel

First published in 2016 by
UCL Press
University College London
Gower Street
London WC1E 6BT

Available to download free: www.ucl.ac.uk/ucl-press

Text © Robert Biel, 2016
Images © Robert Biel, 2016

A CIP catalogue record for this book is available
from The British Library.

This book is published under a Creative Common 4.0 International license (CC BY 4.0). This license allows you to share, copy, distribute and transmit the work; to adapt the work and to make commercial use of the work providing attribution is made to the authors (but not in any way that suggests that they endorse you or your use of the work). Attribution should include the following information:

Robert Biel, *Sustainable Food Systems*.
London, UCL Press, 2016. http://dx.doi.org/10.14324/111.9781911307099

Further details about CC BY licenses are available at http://creativecommons.org/licenses/

ISBN: 978–1–911307–07–5 (Hbk.)
ISBN: 978–1–911307–08–2 (Pbk.)
ISBN: 978–1–911307–09–9 (PDF)
ISBN: 978–1–911307–10–5 (epub)
ISBN: 978–1–911307–11–2 (mobi)
ISBN: 978–1–911307–29–7 (html)
DOI:10.14324/111.9781911307099

Contents

List of figures   vi

1. Introduction   1
2. Searching for a new model of food and farming   4
3. The mainstream farming paradigm – what went wrong   11
4. How systems change: crisis and rift   18
5. Embracing complexity: the earth system, land and soil   30
6. Dialectics of a (re)discovered sustainability   40
7. Political dimensions – agriculture and class struggle   48
8. Towards a new paradigm – practical guidelines   58
9. Regenerating the earth system, working with climate   66
10. Food, imperialism and dependency   74
11. Built systems, biomimicry and urban food-growing   90
12. Autonomy, radicalism and the commons   108

Bibliography   125
Index   143

List of figures

Figure 4.1	A succession of structural regimes in the international political economy, punctuated by phases of low order	25
Figure 4.2	A succession of 'waves' in the capitalist political economy of food, punctuated by phases of crisis	26
Figure 4.3	Food price index (2002–4 = 100)	28

1
Introduction

This book places itself within the traditions and the ongoing activity of UCL's Bartlett Development Planning Unit, and within its research cluster, Environmental Justice, Urbanisation & Resilience.

It draws heavily upon my teaching for the Environment and Sustainable Development Masters. I owe an immense debt to all my fellow Development Planning Unit (DPU) staff, as well as past and present students, from whom I have learned much. In particular I am happy to acknowledge the contribution of Yves Cabannes: together we created a Masters module on Urban Agriculture, and explored the framework for a radical re-definition of the topic. My colleagues Zeremariam Fre and Michel Pimbert also played important roles in the module's subsequent development and influenced my thinking in several ways.

At the same time, I approach this topic as a food-growing practitioner and allotment-holder: the allotment movement and its working-class traditions of self-organisation continue to inspire me.

This is a book about how people can feed themselves into the future, and also about major aspects of climate adaptation/mitigation. I sought to approach these extremely serious topics in a spirit of responsibility. The United Nations Food and Agriculture Organisation (FAO) has proposed the need for a 'new paradigm' premised on 'sustainable intensification' and I felt it was essential to engage with this constructively rather than merely critiquing its 'discourse'.

A core concern of DPU is to address environmental crisis through the lens of the interests of working and oppressed peoples; on this basis, we always seek win-win solutions to ecological-social problems. While such solutions are concrete, and thus specific to each case, they also suggest more general conceptual insights, which can in turn serve to guide new projects.

As an example, we may explore the notion of 'risk'. This cuts across several topics and has a special relevance to food security, notably in the context of extreme climate events.

We could address 'risk society' in a Eurocentric and classist way which exaggerates the role of privileged consumers in driving a food regime more concerned with quality than quantity, but the result could be to increase social polarisation, which is exactly what we don't want. Undoubtedly, consumer pressure over chemical risks plays a positive role in some circumstances – China being a case in point – but we should never lose sight of the imperative to maintain sufficient quantity: the question is how, assuming we abandon chemicals, we can produce *enough* food for the world population.

This is why, rather than focusing too much on the question of whether organic food is healthier, my enquiry displaces 'risk' from the realm of consumption into that of production. The core argument concentrates around two points:

The first point is that the chemical, high-input, highly mechanised system destroys the land. This is an argument made by Karl Marx in the nineteenth century and similarly by the pioneers of the organic movement in the twentieth century. In fact one of the main normative aims of the book is to facilitate a confluence between these two currents: radical socialism and organic farming on the basis of their shared aims. If we take seriously the above argument, we will see that food production, on the current basis, is sure to collapse unless we can realise one of the most radical revolutions in human history. It would be ludicrous to think that a revolution of such magnitude could be radical merely in a technical sense, without being also socially radical.

The second point, which reinforces the first, relates to complexity. Here too, there is a potential confluence between Marxism and organics, for which the unifying principle is dialectics and general systems theory, but it also draws strongly on a dialogue between indigenous holistic thought, ecosystem theory and twenty-first-century explorations of evolution and soil systems. The issue is this: if systems are artificially simplified and homogenised – through a linear and reductionist approach where a few parameters control the rest and you expunge the messiness of emergent order – they become superficially stable and predictable, free of uncertainty or risk. But this is achieved only by incurring *both* unsustainable inputs/emissions (i.e. linear flows: fossil fuels coming in, and greenhouse gas coming out) *and* a loss of resilience/adaptive capacity. In a physical sense, the parameters are reduction to a few chemical inputs and strains of seed, which removes the diverse vocabulary of adaptation.

There is also, crucially, a *political* component of the argument: the very fact that simplified systems are easy to control confers power on the interests which set their ground rules. To overthrow the existing order – for example its corporate-dominated food chains – is therefore a political task, propelled by land/food-related social movements.

By following the implications of this reasoning, we will be not just addressing environmental justice in the *distribution* of risk (which is necessary in itself), but making sure that the interests of the vast majority are central in determining the mode of *production*.

Furthermore, in destroying the dominant circuits, just what are we opting *into*? This is where we can begin to define organics not merely in an unsatisfactory, purely negative sense (as an exclusion of chemicals), but in the very positive sense of a decision to opt into the self-organising properties of complex systems.

Physically, this means the land and plants, animals, fungi and bacteria, in all the web of below ground and above ground interactions which make up a constantly adaptive system capable of self-modifying and self-healing in response to shocks. By embracing the free energy of complex systems, we reduce the energy *input* supplied either by labour (under feudal-type oppressive agrarian societies) or, more recently, by fossil fuels. If we remove this input we automatically remove the entropic output (greenhouse gas, pollution)…and thus the energy equation squares up.

Again, the above has strongly political overtones. Society too has its networks, its diverse vocabulary of institutional responses, its self-healing functions. In our specific case study of the city, we see how this process is actually happening in the present moment.

In fact, in reducing physical input, we do require something more intangible to replace it: human capacity, knowledge, wisdom. This reconnects to a central point introduced by the Utopian socialists of the early nineteenth century: the response to pessimistic Malthusian propaganda about an inevitably deficient food supply is to overthrow corrupt exploiters and unleash the associative and co-operative traditions of the working class.

Recent developments have only reinforced this: knowledge and debate *must* be open-source, a commons. That's why I was so keen, in contributing to this debate, for this book to be open access. I must, therefore, conclude by expressing my thanks to, and solidarity with, UCL Press in their decision to make open access a core principle, one with which I am proud to be associated.

2
Searching for a new model of food and farming

A confession of impasse, searching for a new beginning

There is a sense that the world food system has reached an impasse. Hunger afflicts at least an eighth of the world population (FAO, 2012), mostly in the global South, but also in the North where austerity policies – which respond to crisis by prioritising the interests of the wealthy – leave working people hungry. What is even more serious is that even this damaged 'food security' cannot be guaranteed into the future. International institutions now recognise that something fundamental must change, a realisation embodied in the notion of *paradigm shift* (Graziano da Silva, 2015; FAO, 2011) and further concretised in the form of *sustainable intensification.*

Such recognition is all the more significant since, for most of its history, the UN Food and Agriculture Organisation (FAO) tended to be somewhat unwilling to offend corporate interests. Within the UN system it was mostly the two successive Special Rapporteurs on the Right to Food, Jean Ziegler and Olivier de Schutter, who pushed for a more radical and systemic critique. The latter notably placed his authority behind *agroecology* (de Schutter, 2010), a term that implies bringing farming back to an understanding of natural systems, and that forms an important point of reference for this book.

A landmark in official critiques of the ruling food paradigm was the publication of *Save and Grow, A New Paradigm of Agriculture – A policymaker's guide to the sustainable intensification of smallholder crop production* (FAO, 2011), which argued specifically for a revitalisation of small farms and a recognition of their dignity and essential contribution. Expanding on this, the UN Conference on Trade and Development (UNCTAD) further stated: 'The world needs a paradigm shift in agricultural development: from a 'green revolution' to an 'ecological intensification' approach. This implies a rapid and significant shift from conventional, monoculture-based and high-external-input-dependent industrial production towards mosaics of sustainable regenerative production systems that also considerably improve the productivity of small-scale farmers. We need to see a move from a linear to a holistic approach in agricultural management, which recognises that a farmer is not only a producer of agricultural goods, but also a manager of an agro-ecological system...' (UNCTAD, 2013, p.i).

This and similar statements embody a welcome reflection on what the shift may entail: terms like 'mosaics' and 'regenerative' imply a change in how we think, moving away from linear and reductionist approaches and towards a systems perspective.

These ideas are stimulating. Nevertheless, we should ask whether the new paradigm is correctly framed. Not everyone, even among those critical of the old paradigm, would accept that it is, particularly the assumption that the answer is 'intensification', which could imply a merely quantitative solution and contradict the more qualitative issues raised. Indeed, the notion of a 'new paradigm' entered the debate quite some time ago, precisely in relation to quality issues (Welch and Graham, 1999). The emphasis on quality arose as a critique of earlier mainstream policies, targeting mainly quantity, which often were critically labelled 'productivist' and were typified by the now-discredited Green Revolution in which hybrid crop strains were bred only for quantity of yield.

The question therefore arises as to whether sustainable intensification is merely a cosmetic updating of productivism. Could the problem of feeding the planet be solved in another way?

It might for example be argued (Wiskerke, 2015) that the issue is not insufficient production, but rather cutting waste; indeed, food waste is a crucial issue, commonly estimated to represent between 30% and 50% of food produced (IME, 2013).

Distributive justice as a critique of social ills

Another, complementary, critique would see the problem as one of *distribution*, rather than production. Plenty of food is produced, but fails to reach those in need.

The issue of access to food is by no means just a matter of technical logistics; it is, ultimately, about distributive justice: decent nutrition should be addressed not through hand-outs or largesse, but as a right.

Distributive issues are, in fact, central to political ecology, which critically questions issues like the distribution of risk...of which food insecurity is an integral part.

One way in which the distributive issue can be framed is in the terminology introduced by Amartya Sen (Sen, 1982), according to which malnutrition is caused not by deficient production per se, but by a deficit of 'entitlements' (the means which enable you to access food). And, in the urban context, food justice has an important spatial angle, expressed in the phenomenon of 'food deserts'.

More radically still, we could frame distributive justice in the form addressed by Marx: there is no absolute law saying working people must only be paid the minimum cost of subsistence: we have a right to struggle for a larger share in the value we produce (Marx, 1969 [1865]); and the struggle for improved access to food would obviously be central to this.

For all the above reasons, we might ask if the ruling bodies have an interest in presenting the problem as one of food *production*, simply to distract attention away from the awkward structural issues raised by distribution.

Nevertheless, in the author's view, there are reasons why we might be more favourable to 'sustainable intensification' than the argument so far seems to imply.

The key point is that, although it may *at the moment* be true that there's enough food 'around' (provided we stop wasting it and distribute it fairly), the system which currently produces that food is not ecologically sustainable into the future. It's not just that this system is failing but, more fundamentally, it is actually its *successes* which are eroding our future. This is a point where we can again draw from Marx, who predicted such a sustainability crisis, inasmuch as, under capitalism, 'all progress in increasing the fertility of the soil for a given time is a progress towards ruining the more long-lasting sources of that fertility.' (Marx, 1954 [1887], p.506). We could demonstrate this practically using the case of chemical fertiliser where, with regard to input, there is clear evidence of diminishing returns – between the beginning of the 1960s and the mid-2000s, global fertiliser inputs per hectare increased 5.5 times for a 2.5 times increase in cereal yield per hectare (UK Government, 2011, p.79). With regard to output, nitrogen runoff is a major ecological disaster in terms of ecosystem depletion, which (as revealed by recent research) will retain a persistent effect over several decades (van Meter, et al., 2016), while a very similar point can be made about the long-term persistence of fertiliser-derived phosphorus (Powers, et al., 2016). Marx' point about the long-lasting sources of fertility is further illustrated by research (Klinger, et al., 2016) showing how chemical nitrogen application disrupts the natural symbiotic relationship between plant roots and nitrogen-fixing bacteria (rhizobia).

This is why we need a paradigm-shift in the way food is *produced* and why it is not sufficient merely to address issues of distribution/waste.

In this sense the FAO discourse is correct. However, it doesn't tell the whole story: the underlying problem is the logic which drives the present socio-economic system, i.e. capital accumulation, to which food and farming are subordinated. The circuits of capital's reproduction take precedence over the loops and flows of nature (which should form the basis of a sustainable farming paradigm), and *in the same process* increase polarisation, disempowerment and loss of entitlements. There is a tragic narrative of Indian farmers who get into debt buying pesticides and then commit suicide by drinking them, and micro-credit has been revealed as a contributory cause (Associated Press, 2012). The farmers are being drawn into accumulation circuits which then overwhelm them. Or, when US African-American activists such as Ron Finley (Zocco, 2015) challenge the 'food deserts' phenomenon, this is framed as a challenge to structural issues of deprivation: accumulation has in a sense siphoned something *out of* these regions.

The argument so far suggests two observations:

[1] we cannot fundamentally address food issues without addressing the whole structure of society;
[2] we are nevertheless in some sense *obliged* to do so, since there is, at this moment, a window of opportunity to change the food paradigm while there is still enough food 'around'. We dare not delay food-system transformation under the excuse of waiting for more general societal change, because by then it would be too late.

These statements appear contradictory, but in fact we can resolve the contradiction as follows: build the new food system in a way which, from the outset, embeds solutions to big issues of social emancipation; or, find a way to act immediately, but without losing sight of strategic issues. This is effectively the perspective of many of today's grassroots social movements. The latter often identify with the notion of 'food sovereignty', a term widely employed in many regions of the world, notably the global South.

There is a range of academic debates on food sovereignty (e.g. Bernstein, 2013; Hopses, 2014) which often seem somewhat semantic and formalistic. I prefer here to focus on the substance, which is surely that *food security can't be truly secure unless it's embedded in autonomy*. Any nomenclature identifying a social movement will never cease to be *work in progress*, which is exactly as it should be: you must always encourage the real struggle to critique your conceptualisations. And in some sense, radical social movements are themselves evolving the definition of a 'new paradigm' as we speak, in a dynamic and self-defining way which doesn't have to wait for recognition by official bodies.

In fact, 'paradigm' – in the spirit of Kuhn who introduced the term (Kuhn, 1970) – can't be limited to a mere technical model in some applied field like farming: it implies a change in world-view. But it can be a model of farming which *embodies* such a change in world-view. Many food sovereignty movements (for example in Latin America) have a strong input from indigenous peoples, highlighting the need to resolve the deep issues of alienation from nature and from ourselves. This book contends, as a central thesis, that we can achieve such disalienation by bringing society and nature together on parallel organising principles: those of self-organisation.

'Transition': a challenge to human imagining

A major theme arising from paradigm-shift is 'transition': the process (phase-shift, leap of consciousness or whatever we call it) by which we *reach* that goal.

Here, an important notion is *path-dependency*: any established paradigm acquires an inertia, whereby past choices imply future ones (c.f. Tiberius, 2011). Thus, chemical-intensive agriculture is embedded in a feedback loop: chemicals undermine soil and ecosystem → decline in yield → apply more chemicals → more damage to soil, etc. Such trajectories tend to persist under their own momentum, unless a force is brought to bear. Transition is about breaking that inertia.

The above image may suggest 'force' in physics, but in reality the force is also political. In fact, Political Ecology can unify the two categories (c.f. Gale, 1998): for the ruling system, socio-political power confers an entitlement to physical resources (energy/matter, which in Einstein's formulation are expressions of the same thing), to set these resources in motion (through productive processes, agriculture included), and – by realising a profit from that productive act – to initiate a further cycle at a higher level (both of resources mobilised and social power). And we should be careful not to confuse power with mere repressive brute force: what counts are the *structural* forms addressed by Foucault (2003) and Gramsci (1971), whereby those who suffer from the system are trained to reproduce its norms.

What's encouraging is that the recognition of being stuck in path-dependencies is a prelude to escaping them, and this is true of many issues of personal development, as well as societal ones. But then, we must highlight the agents of change, and also the actual *period* during which paradigm-shift occurs. Here, an important issue is the relation between radicalism and gradualism.

The gradualist side of the transition argument is that you generally can't just switch off an old order and have a total overnight change. Thus, the literature on low-carbon transitions highlights a period of 'messy mix' where two conflicting paradigms overlap (Geels and Schot, 2007; Curry and Hodgson, 2008). In the case of food – which is indeed an integral *part of* low-carbon transitions, for reasons which we address in Chapter 9 – this takes a special form, raising specific and very interesting problems. This is because transition, in this case, means *conversion* (switching from chemicals to organic). The main issues are:

[1] You obviously must keep feeding people during transition, so you can't just smash the old paradigm and leave a tabula rasa; therefore the two systems must overlap. That's the aspect which appears gradualist.
[2] On the other hand, the 'messy mix' in farming is particularly difficult because old and new paradigms are incompatible: for example, chemicals kill off natural predators and pollinators which organic agriculture needs. It's harder to 'mix' organics and chemicals than it is, say, conventional power stations and solar. This is the aspect which stresses radicalism.
[3] For a given portion of land you need a conversion *period* (two years, according to Britain's Soil Association). The reason is that it is not so meaningful to say 'organic' in a purely negative sense of avoiding chemicals, rather what we need is a changed approach to *systems*; the conversion period provides 'time to start establishing organic management techniques, build soil fertility and biological activity, as well as to develop a viable and sustainable agro-ecosystem.' (Soil Association n.d.). The deduction is that a given portion of land needs to *stop* producing for a

while, before re-starting on a sustainable basis; but then, how do we keep feeding people?

Framed in this way, the problem may sound discouraging, but in reality it's precisely when we take a systems view that we start seeing optimistic outcomes. It's the very *interdependence* of systems that opens up win-win scenarios where, for example, food security and climate mitigation/adaptation reinforce one another through benign feedbacks. The point is: if the problem's systemic then so is the solution; if a bad situation is embedded in feedback loops, then – once we break free from these – benign loops will self-engineer. This is true not just of the physical dimension (soil-climate etc.) but also of the social dimension, where in place of the old loops – accumulation circuits sucking the life out of farms and communities – the paradigm-shift in farming may find allies in the wider paradigm-shift in society, for example in the case of Community Supported Agriculture (CSA). And even food-system upheavals, such as food price spikes, could be beneficial if they create demand for change during the window of opportunity before food security faces even more serious challenges (severe drought, loss of pollinators).

The city, our specific case study, can make a key contribution. By contributing more to feeding itself, the city takes pressure off the rural economy, allowing the latter to undertake conversion; there is also much scope, through biomimicry, to re-design cities in a way conducive to sustainability; and benign social networks likewise have great scope for self-organisation.

A key point about transition is that, while it may have a gradualist aspect, *the leap of consciousness must be radical*; we will expand on this in Chapter 6. And so must the agents of change be radical: the mode of production is first and foremost a class system, where vested socio-economic interests resist paradigm-shift, or at best want a merely cosmetic or co-opted form. So it's only the dispossessed who can unblock the situation, initiating the process whereby new loops and alignments begin to form.

3
The mainstream farming paradigm – what went wrong?

Three faces of alienation

To resolve the problem, we first need some understanding of how (at the level of basic world-view) the current bad path-dependency became entrenched. We may speak of three closely-linked aspects:

First, the notion of *dominating or 'mastering' nature*. The 'mastery' mindset arose in the phase of nascent capitalism, from the sixteenth century onwards. The conceptual images were violent and sexual, an issue highlighted in Carolyn Merchant's major contribution to political ecology (Merchant, 1980).

Second, the intrinsic link between 'mastering' nature and *expropriating people*. This in turn had two aspects: within the core (Europe) it is expressed in dispossession of the rural population – and of women, as Merchant shows – as well as enclosure of the commons; with respect to the global South, it is expressed in colonialism. Colonialism was all about an imagined right and duty to exploit *a region of nature which indigenous peoples were allegedly neglecting* (Biel, 2015a). Thus, in eighteenth-century international law, 'when the nations of Europe, which are too confined at home, come upon lands which the savages have no special need of and are making no present and continuous use of, they may lawfully take possession of them and establish colonies in them [...] if each nation had desired to appropriate to itself an extent of territory great enough for it to live merely by hunting, fishing, and gathering wild fruits, the earth would not suffice for a tenth part of the people who now inhabit it.' (Vattel, 1972 [1758], p.45). This issue is still with us, for example in today's 'land grabs': whatever their features specific to the most recent period (e.g. hedge fund investment), in essence they carry forward a process embedded in capitalism from its origins, which had always included these twin themes:

(a) assuming rights over a certain portion of nature, and
(b) crushing the resistance of the peoples whose tradition prescribed a duty to nurture and protect it. This also had the more specific effect of severing agricultural science and technique from the direct producers.

Third, the *repudiation of holism*, and its replacement by reductionist and linear thinking. Reductionism and linearity are really expressions of the same thing, in that to assume a system is determined by only one of its parameters implies a simplified chain of command, or of cause and effect. In its concrete application to our topic, the simplification of cause and effect seemingly made it possible to control farming systems *by homogenising the inputs* (strains of seed, fertiliser). It also connects with the previous two points: if the aim is to privatise and commodify (i.e. enclose) some area of nature (an area of land, knowledge, resources), that area must be torn away from the whole and dissected into bite-sized portions.

These three features are all expressions of *alienation*, which in its narrower economic sense means separating us from the conditions and product of our labour and, in a wider sense, a psychology which cuts us off from nature. It also cuts us off from *the consequences of our acts*...this last point being so important to food systems, where people are deprived of responsibility or knowledge of where their food comes from.

Indeed the history of food provides a very good case of the dominationist/reductionist paradigm, an approach which, once initiated, set in motion a path-dependency wherein each new phase tends to go further on the same route. This explains a paradox of capitalism: while its history is one of constant innovation, there is nevertheless a sense that each innovation simply embeds you further in the *same* trajectory: thus, chemicals → Green Revolution → GMOs, etc.

The Malthusian spectre

The forms of alienation just discussed came in through early capitalism's rapid and cataclysmic overthrow of the old agrarian society. In a way, the ruling-class discourse was lastingly influenced by the experience of that transition and, particularly, by the threat to property and class dominance from popular insurrections of the eighteenth and nineteenth centuries.

An important duality arises here. While alienation and plunder of nature were bad, the destruction of the old society – at least in the case of feudalism in the metropolitan countries – opened up a progressive potential which the mass movement wanted to explore, and the propertied interests wanted to crush. Radical movements sought to resist the imposition of a *new* exploitative system in place of the old one. At the same time, in the global South, there was a still-more-epic resistance against colonial genocide. And although it is true these struggles may have failed in preventing the establishment of capitalism and imperialism, in another sense they were not really failures because they set in motion a tradition of struggle which is still highly relevant to today's transition issues.

The massive disruptions of nascent capitalism posed acute problems to the ruling order: where previously most people had grown their own food, now there was a rapidly-increasing urban population which, firstly, had to be fed somehow and, secondly, was deeply alienated through dispossession from the land. The perfect storm of a proletariat, torn from the old society and lacking a sense of identity or place within a new one, *and on top of this also hungry*, gave recurrent nightmares to the dominant classes.

This nightmare, which in one guise or another has haunted them all the way through until today, found expression in the economic theories associated with Thomas Malthus. His vision was deterministic: food supply could never keep pace with population. Throughout the succeeding decades, proppertied interests have shown a certain duality with respect to Malthus. On the one hand (the part of Malthusianism which appeals to them) his determinism tended to stifle the argument of revolutionaries, namely that people could conquer poverty and famine by overthrowing corrupt exploiters and rebuilding society in a rational co-operative spirit. To defeat radicalism, the conservative argument always needs to rubbish co-operative solutions and, in this sense, Malthusian economics offered a pseudo-scientific rationale for the ideas of seventeenth-century philosopher Thomas Hobbes, namely that removal of political authority would result in a *bellum omnium contra omnes* (war of all against all). While the ruling class genuinely fear such a loosening of social bonds, they also find it useful to *exaggerate* the threat of a falling-apart of society, thus frightening off humanity from the kind of socialistic paradigm-shift which could resolve alienation and exploitation.

On the other hand, the bit of Malthus that ruling classes do not like so much is the pessimism. They must convince others, and themselves, that *they* can solve the food problem. In effect, the modernist drive to food productivism was an effort to conjure away the unacceptable face of Malthus. This would obviously only delay the reckoning because, if the productivist model itself came unstuck (as is happening now), the spectre would rise once more.

Malthusian fears thus remain persistent and, arguably, even gather strength under today's neo-liberalism. Temporarily, during the heyday of modernisation (roughly from the end of the Second World War until the beginning of the 1980s), any notion of 'limits' had been repressed by the presumed omnipotence of a reductionist 'science'. However, the neo-liberal counter-revolution of the 1980s, which put paid to modernism, paved the way for a Malthusian comeback, reinforced in a different way during the same period by the rise of environmentalism, which found Malthus' catastrophist streak a useful representation for the seriousness of ecological constraints.

Today, we therefore find a significant tendency in many commentaries (e.g. O'Hagan, 2015) to view current high-profile conflicts – notably Syria – as manifestations of a *bellum omnium contra omnes* triggered by food scarcity. True, it is an empirical fact that the twin food prices spikes of 2008–11 were strongly correlated with social unrest, a finding promoted with great fanfare – with a view to getting the US State Department to take the threat seriously and build it into their contingency plans! – by the New England Complex Systems Institute (Lagi, et al., 2011). However, this argument requires quite subtle analysis. What is correct is that the unsustainable productivist paradigm had offered only temporary solutions to food supply, and remained highly vulnerable to the ecological shocks (for example, drought in Australia) which immediately triggered the price spikes. What is dangerous is to take this as confirmation of a deterministic Hobbesian-Malthusian outcome whereas, on the contrary, such shocks could equally well stimulate a collaborative response of creative system-change, in the spirit pioneered by the French Revolution (as we will argue in Chapter 5). In this sense, the spectre of disaggregation remains a covert fear, triggering the 'new paradigm' discourse just as much as it did the earlier productivism.

The continuity of ruling-class fear of a hungry mob occasions an interesting paradox. Capitalism transforms production and technology radically and, as Marx and Engels point out (Marx and Engels, 1969 [1848]), it has to *keep on* transforming these, probably at an accelerating rate, or it would die. We see the result in agribusiness and factory farming, which have been transformed in their technology, distribution, investment, trade etc., not once but several times. On the other hand, in terms of the underlying property relations which this whole edifice *protects and serves*, the system remains highly conservative, one might almost say immobile. Although initially the birth of capitalism carried a narrative of industrialists striving to overthrow feudal landowners (and this continued through the struggle over the Corn Laws in nineteenth-century England), in a profounder sense all propertied classes have common interests, and capitalism quickly learned to accommodate with and subsume a conservative, even archaic, order of landowning rather than challenging it. Here, we can signal an interesting parallel between the critique of English landholding made by the Land and Freedom movement (for example, Girardet, 1976) and the analysis of Indian society conducted by Marxist-Leninists in the 1960s–1970s (for example, Bannerjee, 1984). Both reveal how the modernising elite is grafted upon extremely backward structures both in physical landholding and, ideologically, within the worst and most reactionary aspect of what is known as 'tradition'. It was surely one of Marx' great achievements that, in the context of a mode of production which appeared essentially industrial, he continued to stress the fundamental role of landed property. He thus argued that, 'The history of landed property... would indeed be the history of the formation of modern capital', and 'The inner construction of modern society, or, capital in the totality of its relations, is therefore posited in the economic relations of modern landed property...' (Marx, 1973 [1857–8], pp.252; 275).

Given the threat of radical protest, and the perception that it was linked to hunger, what solution could capitalism find? The answer was to seek a scientific fix, and – as tends to be the way with fixes – this was simplifying and reductionist.

Reductionism and the chemical paradigm

In a natural order, given that 'The pollution of one is the meat of another' (Lovelock, 2000, p.6), there is no real entropy at the level of the system as a whole. It is true that, if we take a single animal or plant, its existence as a living entity is reflected in the ability to dissipate entropy (Ho, 1998) so, in that sense, it does indeed degrade its food by excreting it as dung. However insects or bacteria evolve to convert this into a useful input which is welcomed elsewhere in the system. The only truly linear flow therefore occurs when the earth dissipates, into the coldness of space, an energy which is *quantitively* the same as the solar energy which entered in, but with higher entropy (in other words its quality is lower) (Penrose, 2010, p.78–9).

Traditional farming had been strongly embedded within this natural system of loops and flows. Then, with the rise of industry in the eighteenth century, there inevitably occurred the imperative to increase productivity to feed a rising urban population. The question arose of whether this could be achieved by an *intensification of the existing (organic) approach*.

It made a certain sense to say agriculture should be accorded a special status, retaining its organic links to nature, and simply intensifying these in a more 'scientific' way. Embodying this view, the Physiocrat school of French economists believed that agriculture *is* the real economy, industry being sterile and merely transforming what exists (Quesnay, 1888). Here, there is some interesting convergence between the political Left and the organic movement: Malcolm Caldwell, in his critique of imperialism, very much affirmed the Physiocrats (Caldwell, 1977), while the early English organic movement – in addressing what had gone wrong with mainstream farming – similarly blamed industry and finance for imposing on farming a purely economic rationale with which it is incompatible (Conford, 1998). As an exercise in political-ecology fiction, we might devise a scenario where capitalism remained ring-fenced within its own (primarily industrial) sphere, while farming was permitted its own realm where the cycles of nature are insulated from those of accumulation.

Historically, however, such a separation could not endure. The underlying reality was that agricultural landholdings were concentrated through a process of expropriation, and set on a course of total extirpation of feudalism's compromise with village-level commons regimes. The knowledge which drove early capitalist 'scientific' agriculture, *even when still organic in a physical sense*, was already stolen away from the direct producer (c.f. Zelem, 1991) and it was precisely because science was now floating on an elitist plane, cut off from the complex realities of the cultivator, that it fell prey to that reductionist quest for simplistic, single-cause approaches which was already characteristic of capitalism from its inception. In fact, in the Death of Nature argument (Merchant, 1980), there is an intrinsic link between the expropriation of nature via land-grabs (dispossession, resource-grabs, knowledge-grabs), and the reductionist paradigm of science. It was therefore impossible to ring-fence agriculture from the rest of the economy.

The foundations of chemical reductionism were laid in the nineteenth century and at this point, before pesticides and herbicides came in, the main focus was on improving fertility. Everything was reduced to inputs of three elements: nitrogen (N), potassium (K) and phosphorus (P). Among these, a particular emphasis fell on nitrogen, and the great fix was to find a way to manufacture this synthetically, through the Haber-Bosch process (Leigh, 2004), derived from fossil-fuel feedstocks.

The N-P-K idea in itself has a value. In English gardening lore it is enshrined in the mnemonic shoots-roots-fruits: nitrogen is good for leafy crops, phosphorus for root-crops, and potassium for flowering or fruiting crops. Thus, for example, in the case of a home-made organic fertiliser derived from Russian Comfrey Bocking 14 (*Symphytum × uplandicum*), employed by the author, it is helpful to know that it is high in P and K and we may therefore expect it to be beneficial when applied to a crop like potatoes where there exists an inverse relation between the volume of green ('shoots') and of tubers, so you don't want too much N.

Where it becomes a problem, however, is if everything is *reduced* to these inputs. This is what led Justus von Liebig, who in the early nineteenth century first discovered the role of N-P-K, to warn about the fatal risks which would follow such reductionism (von Liebig, 1843). Von Liebig's warnings in turn influenced Marx (Clark and York, 2008; Bellamy Foster and Magdoff, 2000). The error in reductionism is to lose sight of complexity, in this case by failing to perceive the *systemic* sources of fertility. Where traditional farming operated in partnership with complexity, modern farming undermines it.

From this direction, the critiques made by Marxism and by the organic movement are essentially similar. Where Marx foresaw that capitalist agriculture 'leaves deserts behind it' (quoted in Perelman, 1987, p.37), Alfred Howard, the founder of the English organic movement, observed – employing an interestingly socio-political image – that 'the land has gone on strike' (Howard, A., 1943); thus Marxism and organics can converge, which is one of the normative propositions of this book. Since Marx' day, and Howard's, these predictions of soil-destruction have been fully confirmed. With a recognition that soil conservation is 'central to the longevity of any civilization'(Montgomery, 2007, p.6), media interest is now awakening to the fact that soil is disappearing (Hough, 2010), an interesting notion being 'peak soil' (Montgomery, 2008). In fact, soil is vanishing at up to 50 tonnes per hectare per year, 100 times faster than its formation rate (Banwart, 2011), and cannot quickly be replenished (Arriaga, et al., 2012).

The loss of soil itself is one of the profoundest features of what we can now see as a crisis, not just of food systems but of humanity's relations with nature.

4
How systems change: crisis and rift

Demands for paradigm-shift reflect the fact that the reductionist approach we have just described has now reached an impasse. We begin to see a peculiar behaviour that is characteristic of systems which objectively need to change but cannot yet work out how. This is connected with the notion of *bifurcation*: staring at a crossroads, wondering which path to take. Physical systems sometimes hesitate like this, oscillating between possible outcomes, and in one sense human systems do the same. But with human systems there is a crucial difference: the change to a new order won't just 'happen', we must vision it and deliberately bring it into being.

Let us now seek a deeper understanding of how such an impasse is expressed.

Two views on equilibrium

In our discussion of chemical reductionism we used a perspective of thermodynamic flows, viewing systems through the resources which flow into them and the waste they excrete. In this perspective, we would see entropy as 'untucked loops'. This is an important definition, but a bit limited: we also need to understand what is going on *within* the system, essentially its processes of organisation. Fundamentally, the two perspectives converge, in that low entropy permits self-organisation, and vice versa: thus, 'The entire fabric of life on Earth requires the maintaining of a profound and subtle organization, which undoubtedly involves entropy being kept at a low level.' (Penrose, 2010, p.77). However, there are interesting differences of emphasis, notably on how we regard equilibrium, and therefore 'rift'.

Let us first consider the good side of equilibrium. For example, in the soil system there are three loops: nutrient input/release; soil erosion/production; and carbon sequestration/emission. In an undisturbed natural setup these are kept in balance and the result is no erosion (Amundson, et al., 2015). With the arrival of industrial society, however, things were disrupted, leading to linear flows with many untucked loops (c.f. De Rosnay, 1979), of which erosion is one expression. To set things right, we can strive to restore balance – a realisation which led von Liebig to remark: 'Can the art of agriculture be based upon anything but the restitution of a disturbed equilibrium?' (von Liebig, 1844). Another example is the natural equilibrium between insects that might damage our crops ('pests') and their natural predators, an equilibrium destroyed by chemicals. When the author was obliged to leave his plot unattended for a whole month during the growing season, a natural ecology took over: in response to a surfeit of slugs (*Arion hortensis*) lurking in overgrown grass paths, toads (*Bufo bufo*) took up residence. Some Mexican scientists were recently astounded to find that, when a certain farmer stopped using pesticides, a natural ecology stepped in to do the job (Entomological Society of America, 2016); they then invented the term 'autonomous pest control' for something which nature and traditional farmers have been doing forever! Even built systems, as we will see later, can be redesigned, through biomimicry, around loops and flows.

In all these ways, we could say the goal is for things to be integrated and harmonious. Conventional attempts to connect Marxism with general systems theory have tended to focus on this particular angle of thermodynamic flows (for example Burkett and Bellamy Foster, 2006; Martinez-Alier, 2011), and accordingly, in eco-Marxist literature, 'what went wrong' with the advent of capitalism is often expressed in the notion of 'metabolic rift'. This term was developed particularly by Bellamy Foster (2009), who chose to translate Marx' term *Stoffwechsel* (Marx and Engels, 1968, p.198) as 'metabolic interaction' (Bellamy Foster, 2009, p.177) in place of the more usual 'exchange of matter' (Marx, 1954 [1887], pp.183–4).

The above argument, though important, is, however, only partial: the downside is to over-emphasise the *desirability of equilibrium*, and therefore perceive the sense of 'rift' as something bad. That is why we should complement this with the complexity perspective where, in a sense, instead of looking at the flows entering and leaving a system, we focus on what happens within it: self-organising processes.

In this perspective we encounter a different angle on entropy: *too much* equilibrium.

Thus 'We now know that simplicity and stability are exceptions', beyond which we encounter '*an unexpected intrinsic structure of reality...*' (Prigogine and Stengers, 1985, p.216; italic original). The beauty of a system far from equilibrium is that it attains this realm of creative self-organisation where it self-generates structure. This is closely linked to complexity, in that 'A universe in equilibrium cannot be complex, because the random processes that bring it to equilibrium destroy organization' (Smolin, 2013, p.202). In the pre-Socratic Greek philosophy, which strongly influenced the origins of general systems theory in the twentieth century, change and flux are the only absolutes. Therefore, unchangingly stable systems don't achieve much; rather, what counts is the equipment which allows them to regulate their instabilities (c.f. Wallace, 2015). It follows that, when a system's stability veers towards stagnancy, what it really needs is disruptive forces.

This implies a duality in the notion of 'rift'. In the sense of losing touch with nature and, more specifically, of breaking the loops which recycle the waste from one process as an input to another, rift is bad, but, where it means ripping apart a static and outmoded equilibrium, it is good. Imbalance and unpredictability should be accepted as expressions of the dynamic character of systems but, of course, the environmental justice dimension is to avoid their ill-effects being shunted onto the poor and vulnerable.

The juxtaposition of these conflicting definitions of entropy, equilibrium and rift helps explain why the progression of a system through time is not gradualist or smooth, but instead lumpy and marked by qualitative leaps: during some phases stability prevails, at others, disturbance. We notably find such a view central to the work of ecologist C.S. Holling (b. 1930), who showed how systems explore the potential of a particular phase until it is exhausted, whereupon an intense disruption ushers in a new phase (Holling, 2001). The process is cyclical in that such phases alternate in succession, as they do in evolution where environmental rifts often trigger rapid bouts of diversification; evolution is definitely *not* gradualist (Gould and Eldredge, 1977, p.141). Indeed, Holling and colleagues interestingly remark that the image of a nature in delicate balance is *actually Malthusian*; in refuting this argument, they say: 'natural ecological systems have the resilience to experience wide change and still maintain the integrity of their functions' (Holling, et al., 2002, p.19). Indeed, in a sense, the resilient capacity of any system can itself be considered a *product* of the disturbances it faces and surmounts.

Regime shifts and the role of feedback

Although the alternation of order-disorder repeats itself cyclically, the character of each new phase is specific and unlike previous ones. To represent such specificity, we often use the terms 'regime' or 'state' in the particular sense of a 'mode of organisation'.

Let us briefly take the climate issue (to which we will return in more detail in Chapter 9) to illustrate issues of regime-shifts (state-shifts). 'It is now well documented that biological systems on many scales can shift rapidly from an existing state to a radically different state' (Barnosky, et al., 2012) and, of course, we know that 'It is possible that anthropogenic climate change will drive the Earth system into a qualitatively different state...' (Higgins and Scheiter, 2012).

Clearly the kind of state-shift to avoid at all costs is the tipping-point of runaway global warming (our strategies to avoid this are what we call 'mitigation'). However, there are other state-shift thresholds which it is too late to prevent, and which we simply must adapt to...notably the greater frequency or severity of extreme events. In this respect, it is probable that we have fairly recently (i.e. within a generation) embarked on a new era. For instance, with regard to hurricanes, regime shift seems to have occurred in the late 1990s: there are either *more* major hurricanes (Holland and Webster, 2007) or, perhaps, they are less frequent but more extreme (Kang and Elsner, 2015). Such climate regime shifts are now entrenched: thus it has been said that 'Over the next century, all models show a continued trend for more extremes in the temperature-related extremes indices' (Tebaldi, et al., 2006, p.206), while it is increasingly demonstrable that the phase-shift to a warmer climate provides an overarching logic linking seemingly unrelated extreme events (Committee on Extreme Weather Events and Climate Change Attribution, 2016).

The relevance of the above for farming does not need any emphasis. For instance, a threshold has been crossed whereby record-breaking rainfall events, often impacting agriculture, have qualitatively increased since the 1980s (Lehmann, et al., 2015). The empirical confirmation of phase-shift for the author, who has practised food-growing over the past decade and a half, is that there is no longer what we could meaningfully call 'normal' weather.

Here, a crucial point arises. Humanity has always shown a creative capacity to respond to challenges. Traditional farming systems embraced disturbance because it strengthened them, an argument which draws upon the role of immune systems. This is ingrained in our being, because of the way evolution tested us across past ecological difficulties. In this sense, what is commonly seen as an adaptation *problem*, we could more positively view as a challenge to embrace the *opportunities* of a new era, one which demands the kind of resilient, modular, distributed and networked structures/institutions which would be beneficial to society in any case, and make life generally more interesting.

Introducing 'panarchy' – how systems are ruled

Even ecological disasters have historically been harbingers of progressive agricultural change, both technical and institutional, as shown in the research of Thirsk (Thirsk, 1997). However, if possible, we want to avoid major disasters *and this is precisely the reason for embracing lower-level disturbance*. In other words, either we embrace 'normal' disturbance as a trigger for immunity, or we try to block it, in which case it becomes catastrophic. This is an extremely important point.

Berkes and Folke explain the theory behind this when they praise traditional Amazonian swidden-fallow land-management approaches which mimic natural fine-scale perturbations and thus 'avoid the accumulation of disturbance that moves across scales and further up in the panarchy' (Berkes and Folke, 2002, p.131). Let us unpick the meaning of this, because it harbours an interesting duality. On the one hand, 'panarchy' means that a system's site of 'rule' *is situated at the level of the system itself* ('pan' = all) – this is the dimension of holism. On the other hand, the reference to 'further up' draws upon a particular usage of 'hierarchy' (different to that which we might employ to describe a society like feudalism): the panarchy is a set of *nested* subsystems (Holling, 2001), and the point is that if we attempt to stifle disturbance while it is still at a manageable level it will only reassert itself at another, more threatening, level.

So what can we draw from the above to help us understand 'what went wrong'? If we try to control a system too much, *and in particular make it too simplified and predictable*, if we fail to embrace the creative face of chaos, if we homogenise and smooth things out in the interest of predictability…then the system becomes fragile and vulnerable to a more general crisis. '[S]implified intensively managed systems become more inflexibly "brittle" and thus more prone to erratic behaviour (including systems collapse)...' (Rees, 2010, p.2). If we aim for predictability of short-term benefits in ecosystem management, the result will be greater long-term fragility (Carpenter, et al., 2015).

This takes us to the essence of the contradiction within what is conventionally called 'food security'.

In relation to livelihoods, an aspiration to predictability is meaningful and legitimate. People have a right to secure employment, lodging etc. and, in the same way, need to be confident that there will be enough to eat, so in this sense you wish things to be as predictable as possible. That is all fine. But the problem is, if you try to *achieve* this by making the system simple, uniform and standardised, it will have the reverse effect. The Green Revolution and globalisation (which we address in more detail in Chapter 10) perfectly illustrate the wrong approach: in the Green Revolution, you grow only a few crops and a few strains of each, with no variability at all in height or appearance. You still see the legacy of this in the EU's regulations on seed, which distrust traditional varieties because they lack what is called 'stability'. In globalisation, you create an expectation that every vegetable (at least in Northern supermarkets, which form the end-point of global value chains) should be available 365 days a year, and of a standard size and blemish-free. Such false attempts at predictability heighten alienation, distorting how the world really is: vegetables *should* be seasonal, they do not all look the same, and each year is different in terms of which crops grow well. Although the predictability of the Green Revolution/globalisation type *can* be achieved, it comes at an immense and unsustainable cost. Partly this is measured in the physical inputs required: fertiliser, water, herbicide, pesticide; and, more importantly still, in the loss of resilience suffered by any homogenised system. Thus, 'the diversity of responses to environmental shocks is closely related to resilience' (Carpenter, et al., 2015, p.5).

What you lose in the approach which over-emphasises uniformity is the most precious treasure of traditional approaches, which made a virtue of variety, preserving all possible strains of a particular crop (c.f. Shiva, 1988) for the reason that evolved characteristics possessed by each might save humanity in the face of some unpredictable threat. It is precisely the variability of traditional strains, *the fact that they are not 'stable' but keep evolving,* which provides this robustness. Inevitably, the unpredictability which modern reductionist approaches sought to banish returns to haunt us today at systemic level. The very inputs which were supposed to make things more secure now trigger (in the shape of greenhouse gases, nitrogen runoff etc.) a regime of intensified ecological stresses and extremes which a simplified system cannot withstand.

The above perspective, which would enrich political ecology, relates in a subtle way to the more obvious *political* manifestations of control: if we assume the flows of command in a system to be linear and deterministic, with one variable governing the rest, then obviously *political control will be easier*. Again, we see the relevance of Gramsci and Foucault (see Chapter 2): we should always look for the ways in which power over people functions *through control over systems*.

Phase-change: under capitalism and beyond

An interesting paradox arises here: capitalism, while seeking to impose an impossible stability on nature, is, in its *internal* workings, much more keen to embrace disturbance. It has indeed forged its own parody of how systems develop though successive phases or regimes (Figure 4.1), in which we discern a clear analogy with Holling's ecosystem model. Here too, we encounter phase-shifts opening up a new potential, which is then explored for a period until it is exhausted. There follows an episode of stagnancy and decay, followed by an intense disruption, as prelude to a new phase of order, and so forth. In this way, capitalism has its own 'ecology' but, unlike in previous societies, this is divorced from, and antagonistic to, the natural one.

As a representation of this disorder-embracing faculty, Schumpeter coined the term 'creative destruction' (Schumpeter, 1976). And though I happen to find Schumpeter's own exploration of this notion rather weak and unsatisfactory, the concept itself – which is in fact very much in the spirit of Marx (c.f. Schubert, 2013) – has great potential.

The successive phases in the political economy find a specific expression in the food system (Figure 4.2). Such phases can be seen as 'food regimes'. Thus, as with regime shifts more generally, the development of food regimes is not produced either purely out of structure itself or out of agency (c.f. Potter and Tilzey, 2005), but through some interaction between the two.

In today's situation, we often speak of crisis, but how should we understand this? Perhaps at three levels:

[1] *Business-cycle* or boom/bust (*conjoncture* in French). This relates to the fluctuation which occurs within any given accumulation regime. Such instability is 'business as usual' for capitalists, but consequences for working people may be dire – notably in food security terms;

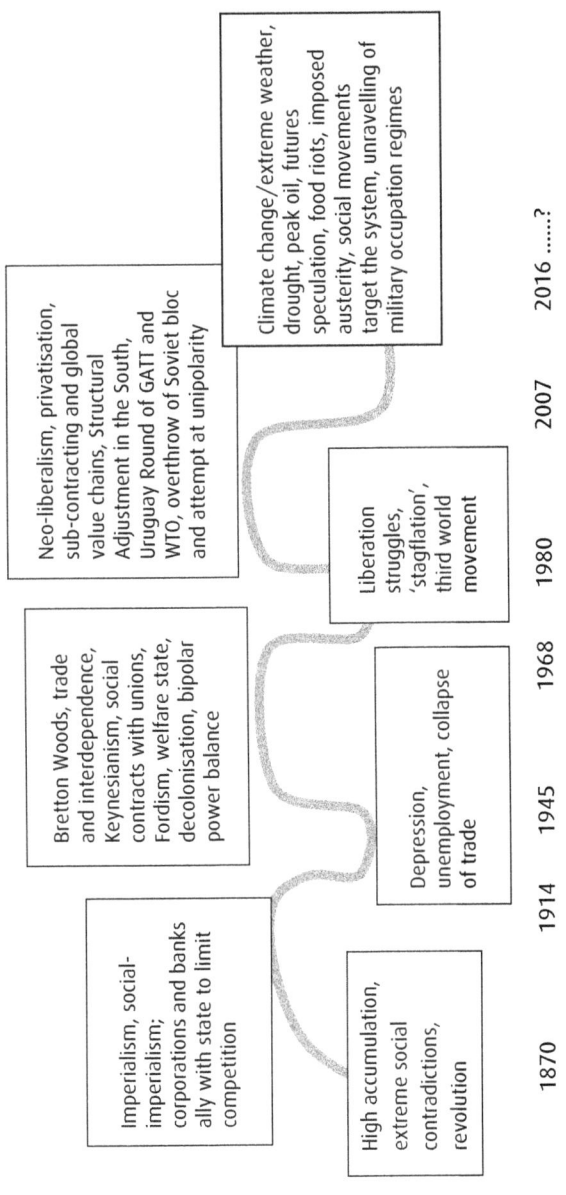

Figure 4.1 A succession of structural regimes in the international political economy, punctuated by phases of low order

HOW SYSTEMS CHANGE: CRISIS AND RIFT

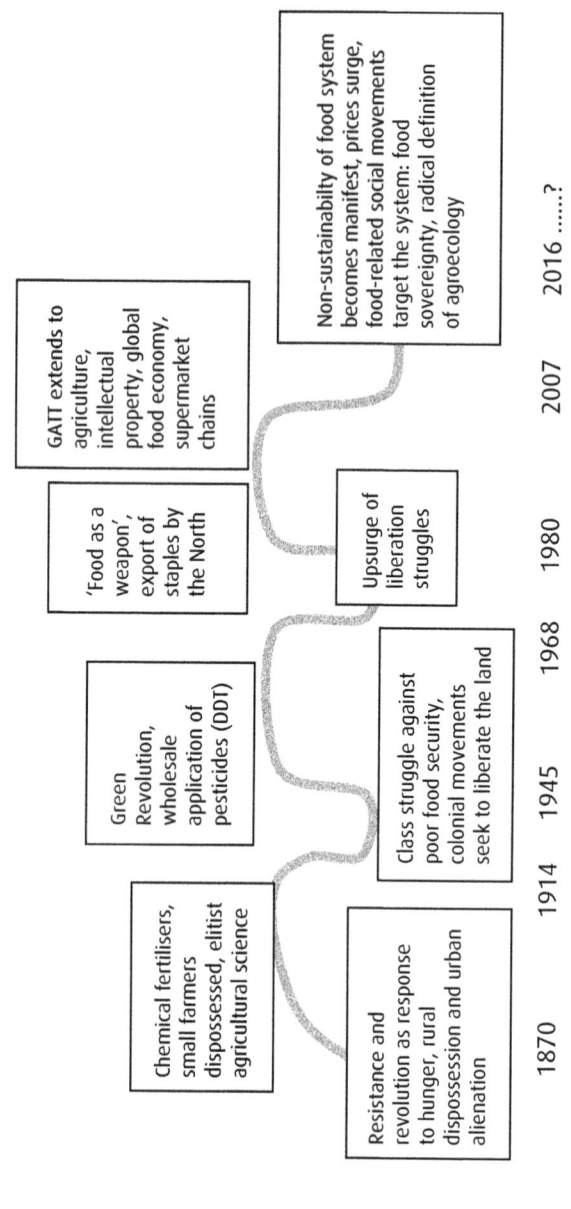

Figure 4.2 A succession of 'waves' in the capitalist political economy of food, punctuated by phases of crisis

[2] *Structural*, in which an entire regime of accumulation comes unstuck. At such periods, it may for a while be hard to see anything 'creative' in the destruction, and even the ruling order is severely troubled;

[3] *Systemic*, in which the whole mode of production is called into question.

The difference between [2] and [3] is not so clear-cut. If we take the case of 1914–45, it was not clear at the time how capitalism would recover at all, and food issues were very much part of this. In Britain, for example, the strong official promotion of allotments extended throughout the *whole* of this period (Acton, 2011) – not just during the Second World War as is often supposed – and can be considered a response to the threat of social unrest from an impoverished and food-insecure working class. It could indeed be argued that most structural crises give the impression of being systemic while you are living through them.

Nevertheless, there are strong reasons why today's impasse may be more profound and more systemic than what went before. A fundamental showdown in humanity's relations with nature has been brewing since the origins of capitalism – effectively nature's revenge on a model which thought it could control complex reality in a simplifying way – but in earlier periods this was merely latent. Today it is inescapable. Moreover, the structural crisis of the neo-liberal capitalist regime of political economy *coincides with* a regime shift in nature (the regime of climate extremes), placing the simplified system under intolerable stress. We may therefore be living through the first truly systemic crisis since capitalism's origins.

In its implications, a new food/farming paradigm therefore requires transcending not just a certain phase of capitalism, but actually confronting a much wider existential crisis of civilisation, culture, psychology and every other mode of being. Radical movements (c.f., for example, Morin, et al., 2012; World People's Conference on Climate Change and the Rights of Mother Earth, 2010) clearly sense this fact. Hence a dualism in the stance of ruling bodies: on the one hand, as in the FAO's conversion to something resembling agroecology, they rightly advocate a new paradigm; on the other hand, they inevitably fear the big strategic implications such a shift would unleash, notably on the part of those radical forces which alone could truly bring it to fruition.

Such a systemic crisis may well have special features, different from those encountered in previous epochs.

There are already certain types of rhythm visible in capitalist cycles. Following our classification above, [1] if we take from systems theory the notion that '...fluctuations rather than stable states are obviously the rule' (Scheffer and Carpenter, 2003), this would be obvious in the business cycle; [2] in the alternance of major accumulation regimes, there is another kind of rhythm driven by a peculiar parody of Holling's cycle of order-exploration and order-distruption; [3] arguably, in a *systemic* crisis, the system has become chaotic. In fact, in chaotic systems there is still a kind of rhythm, which may reflect how they keep hurling themselves against their resource limits and rebounding from these (Gharajedaghi, 2006, p.117–8). Such chaotic behaviour may be visible in the behaviour of food prices from around 2007 onwards (Figure 4.3).

From physical systems we learn that, as they approach a point of bifurcation, volatility is indicative of an impending qualitative shift: 'It is remarkable that near-bifurcations systems present large fluctuations. Such systems seem to "hesitate" among various possible directions of evolution...' (Prigogine and Stengers, 1985, p.14). We could make an analogy with oil prices, which also appear trapped between two conflicting tendencies, namely tendencies to both high and low prices, each of which could be bad for the fossil economy (high by encouraging a shift to renewables; low by destroying the viability of fracking, tarsands etc.) and, on this point, Fred Pierce makes an interesting

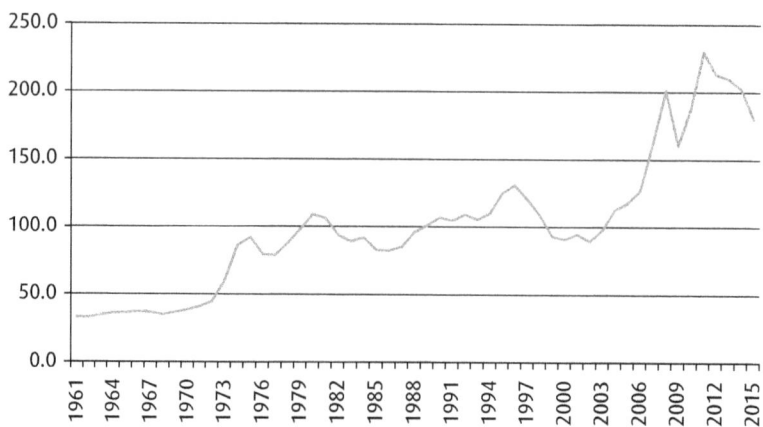

Figure 4.3 Food price index (2002–4 = 100). Source: the author, data taken from UN FAO on http://www.fao.org/worldfoodsituation/foodpricesindex/en/

observation: 'Maybe we are seeing the death throes of our addiction to fossil fuels' (Pierce, 2015, p.23). So, in a similar vein, we could ask if the chaotic features of food indicators herald the death-throes of chemical/fossil fuel-based farming; and whether this in turn signal a wider paradigm-shift in the organisation of society as a whole.

5
Embracing complexity: the earth system, land and soil

If the old system is in its death-throes, where will we find principles for a new one?

What is positive is that systems have a certain capacity to self-organise. This does not of course mean we should sit back and abandon conscious action to create change. It does, however, mean that there is an objective organising force that we can work *with* while exercising our conscious interventions.

We have spoken of self-organisation, but how is this expressed in real terms? If we can answer this in relation to the land/soil, this would also be relevant in redesigning, through biomimicry, our built/urban systems.

Picturing a world of diversity and interaction

As we have argued, a change of farming model must be part of a broader paradigm-shift, a new way of thinking. In nature, everything is about interactions. The flourishing of a single butterfly species requires an interaction between four different biological realms (plants, animals, fungi and protozoa) (Tao, et al., 2015). The whole evolution of forests is driven by complex feedback relations between trees, fungi and bacteria (van der Heijden, et al., 2008). Huge new realms of bacterial life are now being discovered which cannot be studied in isolation because they do not exist in isolation, only in symbiosis with some other form of life (Hug, et al., 2016). Indeed, research now introduces the notion of a 'hologenome', the co-evolution of a host and its symbionts (Shapira, 2016).

Taking this to a conceptual level, 'The richness of the world around us is due, in large part, to the miracle of self-organisation...We're accustomed to thinking in terms of centralised control, clear chains of command, the straightforward logic of cause and effect. But in huge, interconnected systems, where every player ultimately affects every other, our standard ways of thinking fall apart' (Strogatz, 2003, p.43). Complexity is the acting-together of the 'bits' of a system to create something which cannot be reduced to its parts, in that '...complex systems may produce emergent order...without a prescription for the pattern existing beforehand' (Thelen, 1989, p.80). In such a system, Lucas observes, 'We do not understand what will happen in any situation – only that something interesting will' (Lucas, 2005).

This argument is connected in a deep way to Prigogine's re-formulation of the entropy idea (c.f. Grant and Woods, 1995), in that we here see entropy not just as a principle of decay but rather as a stimulus to the self-organising loops which act to *overcome* that decay. As an example, at the level of a galaxy, supermassive black holes (though their internal entropy is high) serve as the force which regulates the entire creative process of self-organisation (c.f. Scharf, 2012). At the level of the earth system, the loops and flows which regulate fertility occur at an immense scale. Thus, the entire climate regime depends on the Amazon, but were the Amazon a closed system it would exhaust itself as rainwater washed away nutrients. It seems that these nutrients are replaced by dust blown in from elsewhere (current research is exploring how far this derives from the sediment of a dried-up prehistoric lake in Chad – Armitage, et al., 2015). Similarly, whales have played a crucial role in shifting huge quantities of phosphorus (an element crucial to plant growth) by feeding at the ocean floor and then defecating on the surface (Doughty, et al., 2015).

Let us now apply complexity perspectives more specifically to the soil. Darwin's thinking was going in the direction of seeing the soil as the foundation for all of evolution, as he homed in on the role of earthworms in circulating nutrients (Darwin, 1881). It is interesting that after travelling the world he ended up in his garden watching worms and, in a sense, he was discovering something important about the systems perspective. Furthermore, worms are only a part of it. Today we also know more about the role of smaller organisms, fungi and bacteria, and more importantly the symbiotic networks – such as mycorrhizal filaments – linking them. Far removed from the paradigm of chemical reductionism, it is the interaction between the soil's chemical, biological and mineral components which is key (Bourguignon and Bourguignon,

2008) and, arguably, the amazing complexity of the biological realm is the most remarkable feature. Fungi were probably the first life on land, and the whole of their existence is wrapped up in symbiosis: even a fungus itself is curiously an assemblage of cells containing many different kinds of DNA (University of Wisconsin-Madison, 2015). The first plants were algae that probably found themselves blown onto land and could only survive by co-operating with a strain of fungi to access minerals (Delaux, et al., 2015). Through these interactions, soil was created, which today includes 100,000 *named* species of fungi and at least ten times (maybe a hundred times) as many unnamed and largely unknown ones (University of Wisconsin-Madison, 2015). There is similar diversity among bacteria: a single gram of soil may include 20,000–40,000 *species* of bacteria, most of which have never been studied (Brussaard, et al., 1997, p.566). Not surprisingly, then, it has been said that 'Soil ecosystems are probably the least understood of nature's panoply of ecosystems....' (McNeill and Winiwarter, 2004, p.1629).

The specificities of the belowground universe are firstly that, although similar to aboveground in the sense that all systems work on similar lines (nutrient loops, feedback etc.), we need a whole new science to understand it. Secondly, it is strongly differentiated from one locality to another. Thus, 'patterns of aboveground and belowground diversity are governed by different mechanisms, which are also scale dependent: local soil biodiversity is strongly driven by spatial heterogeneity, and the diversity of microhabitats found within a single, three-dimensional soil profile *could be equivalent to that found aboveground within an entire ecosystem.*' [our italics] (Bardgett and van der Putten, 2014, p.505). In turn, soil systems are deeply embedded in the feedbacks which regulate the earth system: a large study across European countries showed that, on the one hand, the soil-dwelling community itself needs to be studied as a whole system and, on the other, the functioning of this food web system within the soil is consistently related to ecosystem functioning on a large scale (de Vries, et al., 2013). In all this, issues of scale, spatial heterogeneity and 'nestedness' are central.

Truly to understand plants and the land, science must therefore develop new conceptual tools. This takes us back to earlier pioneers of holistic thinking, for example the notion of 'communities' in the work of Odum (Odum, 1969). Among more recent methodologies are 'trait-based' approaches (Martin and Isaac, 2015) where, in place of the old paradigm's reductionist emphasis on *yield*, we now emphasise the long-term sustainability of crops, *measured by their interaction with the wider ecosystem*. The implications of trait-based approaches might, among other things, go against monoculture, and more generally against productivism. Another useful concept is 'ecosystem multifunctionality' (EMF) which emphasises that even if we switch to organic methods – which is a necessary but not sufficient condition – this could fail if we neglect the wider ecosystem impact (Solon, 2015). What is interesting is the important role, within EMF, of the interaction between aboveground and belowground biodiversity... and the further interrelationship between this and climate (Jing, et al., 2015), the overall biodiversity of a system being strongly correlated to its resistance during, and resilience after, challenging climate events (Isbell, et al., 2015). Or again, we could add the notion of 'adaptive mosaic' (Millennium Ecosystem Assessment, 2005). All the above approaches combine to give some idea of a revolution in thinking, the necessary basis for any meaningful 'new paradigm'.

Most obviously, we cannot 'control' a system of such complexity. This does not mean we cannot aspire to *understand* a complex system, or even influence it, but if we truly wish to, we must think in a different way: one where we do not imagine we can capture the truth by reducing systems to simple components, by assuming one-way chains of cause and effect, or by believing that one particular input (a gene, a chemical) determines everything.

A key feature is the range of processes *connecting* the different parts (this notion will be useful later when we refer to urban food systems, which comprise a mixture of social, biological and built-environment components). Such connections can be represented as networks, and they involve the exchange of information.

Thus, plants communicate through mycorrhizal filaments to trigger pre-emptive response to disease (Fleming, 2014). In an experiment, blight spores were sprayed on a tomato plant and then, after a pause, on a neighbouring plant; the second plant could fend off disease because it was forewarned, through a belowground symbiotic network of roots and fungal filaments, to activate defences (Song Yuanyuan, et al., 2010). Conversely, insects use plants and fungi to communicate. Thus, where plants release toxic defence mechanisms in response to belowground insects eating their roots, aboveground insects are forewarned by volatile chemicals signals, and even leave a 'voicemail' to the next generation, stored by modifying the chemistry of soil fungi (Netherlands Institute of Ecology, 2012). One key tool of evolution is immune systems, which are not merely defences 'against' the environment, but stimulated by it. Thus, as mycorrhizae establish themselves – that is to say, fungi colonise the roots of plants – this triggers a mild defence, like vaccination, to 'prime' plants' immunity and thus improve resistance to subsequent disease (Jung, et al., 2012). In all these ways there is a huge amount of information continually circulating, with which comes a risk of information overload, and an important area of research is to understand how plants discriminate between conflicting signals (University of Washington, 2015).

From this brief survey, we can draw two deductions.

[1] The old paradigm blinded us to the obvious: farmed nature depends on unfarmed. When the FAO speaks of 'sustainable intensification', this means we cannot spread *extensively* by colonising more land, which would not only have an immense impact on climate, but would actually be counter-productive *for agriculture too,* by undermining the wider ecology on which it depends (c.f. Foley, et al., 2011). This is the issue which goes under the economics-speak term 'ecosystem services'. There is more to this, however, than not extending the cultivated area. China for one has been forced to *retract* it, switching land away from cultivation in its 'Grain for Green' programme initiated in 1999, which has already shown remarkable results in increasing soil organic carbon (Song Xinzhang, et al., 2014).

[2] The larger and more strategic point is that we should not simply see the preservation of 'ecosystem services' (i.e. complexity) as a constraint, but rather as an opportunity; not as simply an *external* condition for farming (supplying it with pollinators and natural predators etc.), but as something with profound implications for its *internal* mode of operation: an inspiration for how to learn from, embrace and integrate nature's self-organising capacities. If we make the farmed environment work in harmony with, *and along the same lines as,* spontaneously evolved environments, a new era of sustainability will open up.

The rich potential of co-operation

A complexity approach in our understanding of physical systems also has implications for social systems: it implies something about rediscovering a principle of co-operativity among the many components of a society, and taking this as the basis for our new paradigm.

To create such a benign linkage between science and society, we must first be conscious of an existing *bad* linkage. The metaphors which have been chosen for science have political subtexts. For this reason, the struggle to re-activate our holistic understanding of nature is somehow the same as that to reform the principles of social organisation.

When Darwin was grappling for a conceptual model, he read Malthus and something clicked. The factor he identified centres on the notion of 'struggle', of which there are in fact two forms (Bowler, 1976): between individuals of the same species, and between that species and its environment. The result of Darwin's borrowing led to a certain bias in evolutionary theory, overemphasising conflict at the expense of symbiosis. This undeniably chimed with capitalism's desire to destroy those lower-order movements and utopian socialists who advocated co-operation as an alternative to class rule.

Economic liberalism enters this story in a peculiar way. Malthus is close to Hobbes in interpreting the 'war of all against all' in a sense where the free flow of a system cannot possibly self-generate structure – hence Hobbes' obsession with a sovereign. Darwin on the other hand did (correctly) think that order could arise from a system itself, which is indeed the definition of 'emergence' in systems theory. Liberalism joined him in this but the key point is that both Darwinism and liberalism took a reductionist view, whereby the processes *generating* emergent order were essentially competitive: they therefore retained the 'war of all against all' but, unlike Hobbes and Malthus, it becomes a principle to create organisation, not destroy it.

Two further reductionist distortions were implied in liberalism: [a] the whole fabric of social interaction is reduced to one variable, market relations; [b] the specifically human dimension – intentionality, visioning a desired future, with all the socialistic resonances this may have – is outlawed: an important plank of liberal economics is that any conscious intervention to improve society will lead to a result worse than that generated by the free play of (competitive) market forces. In practice, however, the extremist leanings of these arguments were damped down under earlier forms of liberalism – which retained a certain social and managerial concern – and only burst through in their full horror with the triumph of neo-liberalism, circa 1980.

All these borrowings between science and economics resulted in another feedback loop: first evolutionary theory takes its central metaphor from a highly conservative politico-economic doctrine; → then capitalism (which is in reality killing nature) borrows arguments from this distorted view of nature to make *itself* seem natural; → then this ideological climate reinforces the metaphors of science, and so forth. Because science and society have been so closely intertwined in a bad way, this has the progressive potential that it is not really possible to overturn the old paradigm in one area alone (science or society), without having repercussions for the other. For example, it is hard to think we could restore co-operation in society without also rediscovering a holistic attitude to nature. This is actually quite a strong reason why some hybrid definitions of agroecology-food sovereignty should be seen as an *intrinsically* unified movement for both organic farming and social change: for example, if we understand social co-operation we will have a better mind-set to understand the technicalities of agroforestry, and vice versa. Of course, from the indigenous/First Nations perspective, these categories are not really separate anyway.

Since the Malthusian strand is not just politically reactionary *but also bad science*, it is logical that a counterattack should come partly from within the scientific community itself and, for the same reasons, it is equally logical that this should carry progressive socio-political resonances too. In recent biological theory, the over-simplified and over-conflictual reading of Darwin has been typified by the work of Richard Dawkins who, while correctly arguing for a self-organising universe (Dawkins, 1988), propagated a reductionist emphasis on simple causation and competition, encapsulated in his notion of the 'selfish gene'. A critique of Dawkins therefore helped focus a push from the scientific community to rediscover complexity and holism, and has generated an important literature, including the work of Dennis Noble (Noble, 2006). A particularly useful statement is Brian Goodwin's advocacy of a perspective which 'shift[s] the metaphors that are used to understand evolutionary processes. In Darwinism...the metaphors are of competition and conflict and survival, and in Dawkins' writing it becomes embodied in the notion of selfish genes. Well, from the perspective of organisms as complex dynamic systems...what you find is that organisms are interacting with each other in all kinds of different ways. They are as co-operative as they are competitive...The whole metaphor of evolution, instead of being one of competition, conflict and survival, becomes one of creativity and transformation...' (King, 1996). The *transformative* flavour of this is very much in the spirit developed by Prigogine and Stengers (1984), and the notion that the future is not 'given' (Prigogine, 2003).

Inevitably too, the self-correction of science spills over into a critique of Hobbesian-Malthusian-liberal distortions about social organisation. To reinforce this, let us take an example from an apparently social line of argument, namely Hardin's 'tragedy of the commons' thesis (Hardin, 1968), which could in a way be considered a social equivalent of Dawkins' selfish gene.

Although Hardin's paper is mostly a Malthusian diatribe on population, it makes use of the so-called prisoners' dilemma (PD) model to argue that collaborative efforts will be defeated because it is never possible to trust the other guy, and that actors who work in the common interest are penalised when free-riders grab the benefit of their actions without having to invest the effort. While nominally a social theory (with very strong pro-ruling-class implications of slandering common property regimes), this has implications for science and notably evolution... and has been refuted from within these fields. Thus, Martin Nowak theoretically demonstrates the possibility in biological systems of emergent co-operative behaviours, despite the PD argument (Nowak, 2006). This is confirmed experimentally in quite an interesting context: the *earliest* forms from which it is thought all life evolved already reveal a self-organisation or 'molecular ecology' (Attwater and Holliger, 2012). The research notably shows that 'mixtures of RNA fragments that self-assemble into self-replicating ribozymes spontaneously form cooperative catalytic cycles and networks' (Vaidya, et al., 2012) (RNA [Ribonucleic acid] is an important constituent – and arguably precursor – of life).

The point, I would argue, is not to attack Darwinism per se but to purge it of the 'junk DNA' which drifted into it from the socio-political context of his time. If 'complexity involves an interplay between cooperation and competition' (Baranger, n.d.), the point is not to exclude competition, but rather to recognise that *evolution tends to select for those organisms which are better co-operators*... for the simple reason that co-operativeness gives them an advantage to out-compete their narrowly competitive fellows! Thus, experimentally, 'When such cooperative networks are competed directly against selfish autocatalytic cycles, the former grow faster, indicating an intrinsic ability of RNA populations to evolve greater complexity through cooperation.' (Vaidya, et al., 2012). Similarly, in Noble's research, genes are selected for their ability to co-operate in the larger phenotype, within which each gene may in fact express many different functions according to context (Noble, 2006). Bacteria send out signals enabling the culture as a whole to adapt to its environment, and while (on the PD model) we could expect free-riders to use this information without wasting energy sending out signals themselves, it transpires that, although 'cheaters' are indeed thrown up by mutation, they are continually purged by natural selection. Groups of bacteria (themselves identical, but where the fringe layer is both more exposed to attack and has greater access to nutrients) develop a co-operative way of defending themselves against antibiotics, dubbed 'metabolic co-dependence', which includes an emergent oscillating behaviour which is in some sense a form of 'conflict resolution'. Such behaviour is both *logical*, in the sense that it can be modelled mathematically, and actually observable (Liu, et al., 2015). Bacteria employ the process of 'outer membrane exchange' in order to repair any of their associates who get damaged in some way: 'Social organisms benefit from group behaviours that endow favourable fitness consequences among kin.' (Vassallo, et al., 2015). This research is similarly crucial in understanding the transition to multi-cellular life, where 'Researchers are interested in how the evolutionary transition occurred toward multi-cellularity; that is, how cooperation develops and single cells are not just interested in themselves.' (Wall, 2015). This contrasts with '[T]he Darwinian view [where] each individual is out for themselves' (ibid.). Recent research explores the hypothesis that what drives diversification is *avoidance* of competition: different species evolve through remaining in proximity, occupying microhabitats within a similar niche (Gatti, 2016), a development which cannot be explained by competition. It is therefore not hard to see why, among animals, selection frequently operates in favour of conflict-managing behaviour and, interestingly, game-theoretical frameworks can again be applied in describing this (for examples, see Davis, 1983, pp.108–123, 135–145).

In all this, the point seems to be that somehow *conflict itself acts as a stimulus for co-operation* – in a similar way, we might say, to the sense in which entropy stimulates its opposite, complexity. The above argument will be important for our understanding of symbiosis in nature, from which we can learn as we develop the technical basis of a sustainable farming paradigm. However, we also need to look at the specifically human aspect.

The physical aspect of human evolution has been closely linked with social interaction. Thus, it is at least a plausible hypothesis that the size of the brain developed in association with the process of forming social networks (Dunbar, 1998) but it is not merely a question of the brain's size, because certain types of cell may play a role in social network formation (Coghlan, 2006). It is true that a specificity of human evolution has been that adaptation becomes more a matter of culture than of biology. But here too, we can see processes of conflict-management at work which are, in a way, an extension of conflict-control in the natural world, only now expressed in a cultural form. Conflict is wasteful, and human social systems have developed ways to resolve it (Suliman, 1999); this would apply equally to conflict within societies and between them. This whole argument is interesting in critiquing the 'war of all against all' notion, in the sense that conflict is important precisely as a stimulus to overcoming it. Here, Barkun's analogy between acephalic traditional societies (which lack a sovereign or head) and the international system (which similarly has no sovereign) is interesting (Barkun 1968).

In today's dominant ideology, the linear/simplifying paradigm tries to dominate every sphere, whether we speak of farming or media. Hobbesian-Malthusian ideas are easy to project, and continue to serve, as they always have, to squeeze out any notion of a radical alternative future premised on association. When Wendy Barnaby began researching a book on 'water wars' and was surprised to discover that co-operative responses to water scarcity overwhelmingly outweigh conflictual responses, her publishers immediately withdrew their interest (Barnaby, 2009). Nevertheless, research increasingly reveals how crowds, far from 'stampeding' irrationally, tend to increase their co-operative and rational behaviour in situations of stress or danger (Bond, 2009). Many disasters are known to stimulate heroism and altruism, an argument developed in an interesting way by Rebecca Solnit (Winn, 2009). The 9/11 studies programme of the University of Delaware (Tierney, 2002) shows how not only did ordinary people respond in a constructive and rational spirit to catastrophe, but also that a significant aspect of the relief effort was spontaneously self-organised by them, in contrast to the failed, militaristic and top-down Federal Emergency Management Agency disaster response to Hurricane Katrina in New Orleans.

The 'default mode' – one might almost say 'reflex' – of humanity may therefore be much more collaborative than ruling discourses want us to think, and this could have important implications for future threats to food security. Of course, it is not just about reflexes, but about purposive visioning. And there is in fact an argument that this visioning faculty is similarly collaborative in essence: 'the crucial difference between human cognition and that of other species is the ability to participate with others in collaborative activities with shared goals and intentions: shared intentionality' (Tomasello, et al., 2005, p.1). The above connects us directly to socialism, as well to the co-operative principle with which it has intrinsically been linked, from the utopian socialists onwards.

This has something to do with the relationship between, on the one hand, people as *part* of nature and, on the other, people *reflecting and acting upon* nature. Consideration of this will be the topic of the next chapter.

6
Dialectics of a (re)discovered sustainability

Pathways to a reconnection with indigenous thought

Dialectics refers to a philosophical tradition which can help us understand two key issues: [a] the *substance* of the new paradigm, and [b] the *process* by which it can assert itself:

(a) Substantively, dialectics shows how to transcend the narrow mind-set of linear and reductionist thought and embrace complexity. It shuns a rigid separation of categories and appreciates systems in flux, which is just what a new farming paradigm requires.
(b) The coming-into-being is embodied firstly in the principle of the negation of the negation – the 'new' paradigm is also a *re*discovery of indigenous farming practices, reasserted in the overthrow of capitalism-colonialism – and secondly in the 'leap of consciousness' required by transition.

A focus of this book is to bring radical socio-political thought closer to organic agriculture. Although, as methodologies, the organic movement might refer to systems theory, and Marxism to dialectics, in reality the two have much in common. In fact, from its origins in the 1930s, systems theory drew inspiration from the pre-Socratic philosophers (Drack, 2008), the same source which inspired Hegel in framing the dialectics which Marx subsequently developed. To emphasise these parallels, we need only juxtapose Hegel's remark (in his lecture on the leading pre-Socratic thinker Heraclitus), 'It is a great advance in thought to pass from Being to Becoming' (Hegel, 1995) with Prigogine and Stengers' remark that non-equilibrium systems reveal 'a glimpse of the road that leads from being to becoming.' (Prigogine and Stengers, 1984). When general systems theory says '...fluctuations rather than stable states are obviously the rule...' (Scheffer and Carpenter, 2003), this sounds exactly like a quote from one of the pre-Socratics who, in turn, were drawing upon ancient Asiatic knowledge systems. This takes us back to the source: the indigenous approaches upon which we must draw as the practical inspiration for sustainable food growing. For the pre-Socratics, nature itself *was* the paradigm for dialectics; similarly Engels pointed out that his and Marx' dialectics were always a reflection of the real world, rather than an imposition of some theoretical framework upon it. It is most interesting that Engels chooses – to illustrate the embedding of dialectics within nature – examples from plant evolution and soil structure (Engels, 1969 [1894], p.162–4).

If dialectics is *about* ceaseless change, it must itself practice this, ceaselessly testing and enriching itself by confronting its own weaknesses. In their time, Marx and Engels were breaking fresh ground, and only by taking dialectics beyond the point reached by Hegel could they generate new propositions on the relations between matter and form (Günther,1964, p.271). Furthermore, as Wan shows (Wan, 2013), Engels' quest to break from reductionism and restore holism led him to insights which anticipate the notion of emergence in systems theory (c.f. Wan, 2013, p.429). And then Lenin, when he in turn addressed the legacy of Marx and Engels (Lenin, 1972 [1908]), realised that this voyage of unending discovery must continue: however farsighted Engels' work, it is not a question of science 'coming round to' truths 'revealed' by him, but rather, with each new scientific advance, we question existing definitions of dialectics. A revision of Engels' own propositions is therefore 'demanded by Marxism' (Lenin, 1972 [1908], p.300). Of course Lenin was writing when there were just the first inklings of what was to come in terms of relativity and quantum theory.

While the above emphasises constant advance and innovation, there is also, embedded within dialectics, a theme of *return*: to the wisdom of a time before we got side-tracked by reductionism. It's this relationship between innovation and rediscovery which is the soul of the negation of the negation.

The general explanation of this concept is as follows:

[1] The 'other' from which you demarcate yourself is the main bestower of your own identity: we see this in Spinoza's 'every determination is negation' or, in the form developed by Hegel, 'What something is... it is wholly in its externality' (Hegel, 1969,

p.528). In systems jargon, a system's identity depends on the area from which its boundary separates it and which determines it negatively (Zwick, 1983); from another angle, there is the 'skin' within which a living being maintains low entropy (Ho, 1998). Such a perspective is central to Hegel's great work *The Science of Logic* (c.f. Hegel, 1969, p.106).

[2] But this 'other', against which you posit your identity, cannot be eliminated, because then your own identity would cease! Therefore, the thing negated is (in Hegel's term) *aufgehoben*: 'sublated' or preserved-in-the-act-of-destruction. When the new stage is in turn superseded (negated), this liberates the negative determinant which it held imprisoned within it.

The 'messy mix': where new and old overlap

Translating this to our case, we have two successive moments:

[1] The scientific paradigms installed by early capitalism, and exemplified by Francis Bacon (Merchant, 1980), turned their back on holism, replacing it with reductionism, mechanistic and linear notions of cause and effect, and a violent aspiration to control nature, ignore its constraints and bend it to our will. The *agricultural* model was a direct reflection of this, as we have seen. On this basis, there occurred the modernist/capitalist rift, antagonistic to nature. However, modernism could not fail to pay tradition the compliment of continually attacking it, as its own negative determinant.

[2] Now, in the process of striving for a new paradigm (an indispensable part of which is radical political struggle), the first rift is repaired by a second, through which we tear ourselves free from capitalism. In this process the indigenous approach – holism, stewardship over nature, organics – reasserts itself. Of course, this does not simply mean turning the clock back because, as Heraclitus says, you do not step in the same river twice. Thus, biomimicry is not only the basis of traditional farming approaches (intercropping, agroforestry), but *also* the cutting edge of today's science of materials, or industrial design, an issue we will address in Chapter 11.

The breakthrough came when it was (partially at least) realised that the Baconian paradigm was bad science. As Capra points out (Capra,

1992), the scientific revolutions of the early twentieth century actually take us back to the ancients (and effectively, I would say, to indigenous thought): things like the quantum wave-particle duality (see Chapter 9), mind-boggling to mechanistic thinking, would not faze a traditional sage. And as we have seen (Chapter 5), today's academic soil-ecosystem research is often infused with the same respect and awe for nature's properties that the ancients had.

Should we then conclude that Merchant's critique of the distorted world-view of early capitalism (Merchant, 1980), however brilliant as a historical study, is flogging a dead horse with respect to today's situation? The answer is no, because in the real world, transitions necessarily occur in a confusing way, with parts of the process overlapping and out of synchronisation with others. We might see this as an expression of the 'messy mix' (Geels and Schot, 2007; Curry and Hodgson, 2008) mentioned earlier. Notably, corporate interests, part of imperialism, remain highly conservative, a fact nowhere better expressed than in the mainstream farming paradigm, whose dominance is scarcely shaken by all the evidence that its whole foundation is wrong. Here, linear and reductionist approaches, which are wholly out of date in scientific terms, still pass themselves off as cutting-edge: this has been the story from the Green Revolution right through to many aspects of today's biotechnology.

We will examine the imperialist basis for this in Chapter 10 but, at a conceptual level, the weird contradiction between scientific progress and reaction is one which Marxist analysis very much predicted: the progress back/forward to a (re)discovered dialectics is *itself* dialectical. In other words it is not smooth, linear or uniform, but rather uneven and lumpy, and notably punctuated by reactionary interludes.

Thus, in the *Dialectics of Nature*, Engels describes how, alongside the immense achievements of post-Renaissance scientific revolutions, came a damaging *reactionary* step: a static and ossified world-view. This world-view was pathetic compared to that of the ancient Greeks [or in fact, I would say, the indigenous perspective, one form of which was transmitted through the strong influence of Asian thought on the pre-Socratics], with their understanding of emergence from chaos and of the eternal cyclical flows of matter in motion (Engels, 1954 [1873–83], p.25). Such stale and static perspectives still ruled science teaching in Engels' day, but were (he said) being challenged by actual discoveries, including evolution: such discoveries had the effect of restoring an outlook where nature 'has its existence in eternal coming into being and passing away, in ceaseless flux, in unresting motion and change' (Engels, 1954 [1873–83], pp.30–1).

However, while Engels was right that research advances were pushing *in the direction* of such a rebirth of dialectics, something was also holding it back.

Thirty years after Engels, this was explained by Lenin, as he described the development of a physics which 'is making for the only true method and the only true philosophy of natural science not directly, but by zigzags, not consciously but instinctively, not clearly perceiving its "final goal," but drawing closer to it gropingly, hesitatingly, and sometimes even with its back turned to it. Modern physics is in travail; it is giving birth to dialectical materialism.' (Lenin, 1972 [1908], p.378). In this statement, Lenin surely draws inspiration from a similarly dialectical passage from Marx' *Eighteenth Brumaire of Louis Bonaparte*, according to which revolutions 'criticize themselves constantly, interrupt themselves continually in their own course, come back to the apparently accomplished in order to begin it afresh, deride with unmerciful thoroughness the inadequacies, weaknesses and paltrinesses of their first attempts, seem to throw down their adversary only in order that he may draw new strength from the earth and rise again, more gigantic, before them, recoil ever and anon from the indefinite prodigiousness of their own aims, until a situation has been created which makes all turning back impossible, and the conditions themselves cry out: Hic Rhodus, hic salta! (Here is Rhodes, leap here!)' (Marx 1969 [1852], p.401). This all looks very much like evolutionary learning.

The issue here is that paradigm-shifts are not easy. They are neither easy in theoretical terms, because of the leap of consciousness required, nor in practice, because of hindrances and setbacks encountered in class struggle. In fact consciousness and the practical movement develop hand-in-hand because each requires the other. This is indeed what we see today with food sovereignty: it is both a practical movement and one of conscientisation, the two being inextricably associated, as a kind of liberatory self-education in practice of the type advocated in the radical pedagogic work of Paulo Freire (c.f. Freire, 1972).

We can address the dialectic between objective change and consciousness through the following logic:

[1] As we saw in Chapter 5, the process of self-organisation and order-creation *needn't be purposive*, it just happens.
[2] However, in a human system, consciousness is decisive. The specifically human form of emergent order is more than just a prolongation of processes embedded in the general fabric of life, there is also the visioning of possible or desired futures;

the supposed neo-liberal (laissez-faire) 'refutation' of purposive action is simply a trick to bolster ruling-class dominance.

[3] Consciousness *itself*, however, is a natural process of self-organisation, of the mind, and therefore itself partakes of the objective order-creating process which it describes.

It is this third step which is actually crucial in dialectics: it is about (re)training how we think. So dialectics is a technique: our brain being *itself* a complex system, which we are employing to contemplate complexity, why not initiate a dialogue between the two, between the medium of exploration and its object? Can we *think* in an 'organic' way? Dialectics is rather like applying permaculture design to the mind, getting it to function like the natural system which in fact it is...including its 'Hic Rhodus' leaps into new regimes of organisation.

In this way, we cultivate a situation where order is only relative, things remain in flux, and above all we retain the ability to access the creative facet of chaos.

The realm of conscious visioning

So does emergent self-organisation mean getting things to march 'in step' like a Nuremberg rally? The systems literature seems ambiguous on this. Thus many discussions (for example, Strogatz, 2003) relate to systems where self-organisation is manifested in things moving 'into sync'...as when fireflies spontaneously co-ordinate flashing their light. We could take fractals as an example that occurs often in nature...yet this is not diverse at all, which is actually the whole point of fractals, and in Michel Baranger's explanation, complexity ceases in those regions of a system where chaos becomes fractalised (Baranger n.d.), i.e. too patterned. In contrast to such a uniform-ising definition of self-organisation, the earth-system (Gaia), as well as its subsystems – in particular the soil – are highly diverse.

Here we encounter a very important concept: 'criticality'. A system functions best when it is neither too disordered, nor rigidly ordered. Brian Goodwin puts it well: '...you shouldn't have too much order. You shouldn't have too much chaos. Perhaps you should be at the point where you can move backwards and forwards between the two...' (King, 1996). Criticality means the region of poise between the two. Bateson interestingly spoke of an 'ecology of mind' (Bateson, 1972), and we are always learning more about its analogies with other ecologies. It has actually been argued that a community of bacteria operates like a brain (Prindle, et al., 2015), while the self-repair facility of chloroplasts in plants is similar to how the brain deals with its degraded components (Salk Insitute, 2015). Applying this to consciousness, there seems to be a kind of *frontier* (criticality) between the two definitions of emergence, i.e. the point at which *organisation becomes something other than simply marching in step*; a point interestingly made in recent research about sheep (!) who exhibit phases of dispersion alternating with ones of consolidation and mimicry (Ginelli, et al., 2015).

But the realm of consciousness takes this notion of criticality to a higher level. Thus, 'A key difference between inanimate and conscious objects is that for the latter, too much integration is a bad thing: the piston atoms act much like neurons during a seizure, slavishly tracking one another so that very few bits of independent information exist in this system. A conscious system must thus strike a balance between too little integration (such as a liquid with atoms moving fairly independently) and too much integration (such as a solid). This suggests that consciousness is maximised near a phase transition between less- and more-ordered states.' (Tegmark, 2014). Or, to express this slightly differently, consciousness arises at some critical point between monotony and chaos (Schulz, 2016); it is itself an issue of organisation, a phase transition, lying at the creative point where the freeness of a disordered system meets organisation (c.f. Tegmark, 2014, p.28).

I would argue that such research constitutes both a vindication of the project begun by Engels and Lenin – a bridging of the scientific revolution and dialectics – and an ongoing development, which challenges us to develop dialectics beyond the point which they attained.

Such a project was tragically interrupted in the Soviet Union during the Stalin period, but there are some hints that, in the 1960s, the Soviets were beginning to pick up the threads, with a particular focus being cybernetics. Thus, in a lecture at Leningrad University in 1960, L.A. Petruchenko argued: 'The contradiction between information and entropy, between order and disorder may be regarded as the basic contradiction of the cybernetic system…(seen from here) the principle of feedback…possibly represents a sort of dialectic movement.' (Petruchenko quoted in Günther, 1964, p.274). Similarly, E.V. Ilyenkov, whom I would see as one of the Soviet researchers of the 1960s whose work has retained most relevance today, strongly emphasises, in his interpretation of Marx, how the latter elucidated capitalism from the standpoint of what is common to the operation of *all organic systems* (Ilyenkov, 1982 [1961], p.116).

Such arguments, relating to the frontier between order and disorder and the fundamental meaning of organic systems, invite us to apply them to sustainable agriculture; we will also return in Chapter 12 to considering the socialist experience in this regard. The point for now is that systems thinking, a pathway to overthrow the dead mechanistic paradigm and unify science with dialectics, has clear political overtones. Fundamentally, 'organics' is not just a chemical-free gardening tool, but a view on both the universe and our own social future.

7
Political dimensions – agriculture and class struggle

As a prelude for attempting (in Chapter 8) to sketch out some elements of a practical approach to farming, let us first define a political framework.

The weight of history: good and bad sides of 'tradition'

We have just discussed determination-by-negation. How, then, does this apply to the relationship between farming and the 'wild', between our modifications of nature and the thing itself?

In fact there is a good way and a bad way of exercising such determination. The good way (which we address in Chapter 8) is just to recognise that, by the fact of our very existence within nature, we are modifying it: it is not pristine but our responsibility is to modify it in the right spirit. The bad way is the modernist or colonialist attempt to break free from alleged *'subservience'* to nature, and hence to escape the 'tradition' which maintains us in that subservience. In effect, modernism considers the very notion of awe (wonderment) as somehow dangerous.

In its colonial form, modernisation – in an extension of the sexual images employed in the Death of Nature, as analysed by Merchant (1980) – spoke of 'virgin' land which indigenous people were not fit to make use of, and which the colonisers had a right/duty to grab (Biel, 2015a). The USA's founding myths have much about frontiers, pioneers and homesteaders, taming nature (c.f. Coeurdray et al., 2015) while also killing indigenous people who were trying to stop them. We saw that there are two complementary definitions of entropy: timeless stagnancy (too much order and rigidity), and featureless chaos (too little order). In a sense, *both* these determinations were imposed, by the colonial/

modernist/industrial-urban project, upon the indigenous 'other'... an 'other' from which that project sought to escape, but which it was condemned to harbour always, sublated in its bosom, the detested guarantor of its very identity. From this, sustainable farming will eventually break free as a negation of the colonial/modernist negation, ready to take us back/forward to sustainability.

An aspiration to learn from indigenous/traditional approaches is visible in many of the 'movements' (sets of principles) which have been proposed as pathways to sustainable farming. These could include agroecology, natural systems agriculture, permaculture, low impact sustainable agriculture, regenerative organic agriculture, biodynamics, the Fukuoka system and more.

As a guide to approaching these, I would suggest the following three principles:

[1] In a technical sense, even while each may have its own particular areas of strength (for example, in permaculture we might highlight *rift and margins*; in agroecology *farming in society*, in biodynamics *microbial stimulation*, in Fukuoka *the critique of work*, in natural systems agriculture *working with evolution*, etc....), they nevertheless share a common core. The author's practice has been a pick-and-mix approach without being dogmatically confined to one particular 'ism', and if it's true they are fundamentally compatible, the result should not be eclectic in a bad way.

[2] They all owe a debt, even if not always fully acknowledged, to the historical legacy of indigenous systems, and in fact, this stuff is just what many indigenous farmers were/are doing anyway without necessarily calling it by the name of some methodology. Alfred Howard was inspired by Chinese tradition in rediscovering organics (Howard, 1943). There was a very important counter-modernist re-appraisal of traditional farming, drawing particularly on Africa, in the exemplary work of Paul Richards (Richards, 1985). Permaculture originated in Australia, taking significant inspiration from aboriginal societies (Holmgren, 1990). Native American legacies constitute an amazing source of inspiration, upon which we draw extensively throughout this book. Much of the sustainable methodology can therefore be derived from a mixture of historical, anthropological and archaeological studies of these experiences but, above all, through a respectful learning from contemporary grassroots farmers and

indigenous movements, insofar as they articulate their own definition, *and, most importantly, ongoing development*, of traditional practices.
[3] The technical side cannot be divorced from the politics, and this is precisely where some of the 'isms' fall short. The author attended the International Permaculture Conference in London in September 2015 without hearing any mention of social movements for food sovereignty or land rights. This is why we are placing the current chapter – whose theme is more political – *before* discussing the technique.

A key aspect of our dialectical perspective is the unity of opposites, and it is essential to apply this to what we call 'tradition'. Just because we may hate the modernist slander of 'tradition', it does not mean we uncritically take on board everything: there is a duality within it. As I will now argue, this is relevant to the way we relate to nature and the wild and, in particular, how we intervene in it.

Some traditional societies were more stratified, centralised and *ruled*, in the sense of an order imposed from the centre-top. In contrast, I'm tentatively employing the term 'deep tradition' to represent something closer to the indigenous principle where order is emergent from the panarchy. Even if, as we will argue in a moment, the concrete reality of pre-capitalist (pre-colonial) societies was usually *mixed*, nevertheless the distinction is useful analytically, most importantly because the aspect of society which was more 'ruled' is the one geared to organising *work* and this in turn has big implications for how we intervene in nature, as we will now see.

A critique of work

Let us consider, conceptually, 'work' and its relation to energy. Obviously, food systems must supply more energy in calories than they absorb in labour: a hunter could not spend more energy chasing an animal than is obtained from eating it. Traditional farming systems necessarily obeyed similar constraints: their calorific input-output ratio was strongly positive (Glaeser and Phillips-Howard, 1987). At the simplest level, this gives us one rationale for a low-work system. But the argument for reducing energy input also goes deeper.

It is true that much of what is wrong with contemporary food systems is the waste and pollution *ejected from* them (nitrogen runoff;

greenhouse gases). However, what is ejected is actually a degraded form of what flows in. To express this in thermodynamic terms (c.f. Dincer, 2002), the inflow represents an ordered and useful form of energy/matter (sometimes called 'exergy' or 'negative entropy'), which is degraded into entropy when it is used up. This connects with the theme of transformation or metamorphosis, an important representation of 'flow'. Therefore, the solution to many systemic problems could be cutting input.

In today's mainstream paradigm the input is fossil fuels and chemicals, but even physical work like digging is actually just another form of energy. The transition to carbon simply occurred when the exploitation of physical labour could no longer meet industrial energy demands (c.f. Mouhot, 2010). So I would argue that performing too much work on the soil, even digging or ploughing without fossil fuels, is reflected in entropy. This happens because the free energy of self-organising complexity is lost when we intervene aggressively, mashing up grazing organisms or mycorrhizae and destroying soil structure, and thereby causing water runoff, leaching of nutrients, and greenhouse gas emissions.

The fundamental argument for no-till farming (c.f. Dowding, 2007) is that you operate alongside the soil's own properties, not against them. Empirically on my allotment-site, most people waste both time and energy digging and ploughing, causing loss of fertility; they then inject further inputs in the form of fertiliser to compensate. In the worst case they use petrol-driven hand-held ploughs and chemicals but, even where labour is manual and fertiliser organic, the same logic applies: the more work you perform, the worse the result. Many people abandon their plots because they do not have the time/energy to do all work they imagine is needed. If we simply realise that we will get better yield with less time/work, this could open a new horizon of small-scale high-productivity farming, leaving people space to maintain a diverse livelihood strategy.

The above is not an exhaustive demonstration of the benefits of no-till, which are manifested particularly with respect to climate (e.g. Wang, et al., 2011; Davin, et al., 2014), an issue we will develop in Chapter 9. The point here is just to stress the 'less-is-more' argument.

Of all the modern sustainability approaches, Masanobu Fukuoka's 'do-nothing farming' (Fukuoka, 1978) most strongly highlights the negativity of work. But it is important to emphasise that 'do-nothing' does not mean non-action: the reduction of *work* (physical energy) is coupled to an increase of knowledge. Hunter-gatherers possessed immense funds of knowledge (Goonatilake, 1984, p.4); they 'did nothing' to nature but were in effect harvesting knowledge. In farming, while physical work (e.g. ploughing) is negatively related to the free energy of the complex soil system, knowledge is positively related because it strengthens the soil's self-organising capabilities. It achieves this by, for example, mulching, using such forms of biomimicry as intercropping, or in the case of Fukuoka's system broadcasting seed-balls containing many varieties of seed and allowing nature to decide which would germinate where.

The implications of this argument are by no means confined to a critique of capitalism; they go right back to the dawn of the so-called agricultural revolution. Wherever centralist/top-down agrarian systems conducted large-scale interventions (irrigation in place of water-conservation, monocropping in place of intercropping, deep ploughing in place of conserving soil structure, plantations in place of sensitivity to micro-characteristics of particular fields), they effectively increased entropy expressed as a deficit of self-organisation.

How farming structure may relate to yield

On this basis, a hypothesis suggests itself: there existed, among pre-capitalist agrarian societies, some correlation between, on the one hand, farming systems closer to self-organising nature (i.e. the indigenous principle or deep tradition) and, on the other, socio-political systems which were relatively less stratified or exploitative and gave more scope to *societal* self-organisation. Conversely, there is an association between invasive, monocropping systems and class stratification. To explore this fully would be a project in its own right, but it does suggest some interesting lines of enquiry. If it were true, the class dimension could then be expressed in a conflict *between two definitions of organisation*:

(a) On the one hand, approaches that are not scared of self-organisation, are open to exploring the criticality between order and disorder, and are thus resilient in the sense of being able to self-modify in response to shocks.
(b) On the other, a centralised, top-down approach where society/production was (is) organised by elites. This relates to our earlier point about trying to make systems predictable by simplifying them and instituting linear chains of command. Such systems need to be organised, and this legitimises the elites whose raison d'être is to do just that: if they can do it for farming, they can also do it for society. In a certain sense, class society increases work *because it can*.

Marxism is strong on emphasising the continuity of class struggle across the whole history of stratified modes of production (c.f. Engels, 1970 [1877]), which raises an extremely important point: our 'new paradigm' must settle accounts not just with capitalism, but with the entire history of exploitation. This truth is nowhere more evident than with food/land issues, where it would be totally artificial to separate today's social movements from the millennial span of peasant struggles. The organic movement is much less explicitly political. Nevertheless, it can be argued that alternative agriculture approaches – whether we call them agroecology, permaculture, biodynamics or whatever – are making a *tacit or implicit* political statement whenever they identify with those methods (intercropping, perennial crops, water-harvesting, agroforestry) which are sharply differentiated from the ploughing, irrigation and monocropping more typical of centralised class societies. This implies a dialectical and critical view on tradition which may arguably place the organic movement closer to Marxism than it might realise.

An interesting experimental demonstration that less exploitative systems are more productive can be found in an project initiated by P.J. Reynolds in the 1960s–70s at Butser Farm, Hampshire, England, whereby he replicated pre-Roman Celtic farming practices. The link with intercropping and gathering in Reynolds' work is striking, in that he highlights the lack of uniform height among traditional strains, while at the same time noting that spontaneous plants become effectively incorporated as a key component in diet (Reynolds and Shaw, 1999). The significant finding is that this experiment obtained yields higher than any achieved in Britain prior to the end of the Second World War (Reynolds, 1985, p.406): in other words, the subsequent imposition of Roman slave plantations and feudalism *led to a decline in yield*. It was only the post-war influx of chemicals and fossil-fuelled machinery which retrieved pre-Roman yields... of course in a totally unsustainable way.

Having emphasised the 'deep time' of the class issue, we must nevertheless understand key ways in which centralised agrarian societies *did not* complete the rift from nature, and therefore things got qualitatively worse with capitalism.

Where capitalism made things worse

Firstly, however much traditional rulers substituted work for complexity, this took the form of labour not fossil fuels. Consequently, since the energy of farmers came from the food they themselves grew, the system could not be in calorific deficit. Secondly, even systems like feudalism did not entirely cancel out local self-organisation but rather compromised with it: elite rule was superimposed on a village system of commons regimes, oral knowledge, seed-selection and experimentation.

If the above was true even under European feudalism – which, following Amin, we could regard as a pretty lousy subset of 'tributary' modes of production (Amin, 1980) – it would be even more interesting to look at those non-European societies where elites appear to have subsumed elements of 'deep tradition' and generalised them. For example, in the Aztec empire, we find a farming model organised around *chinampas* or raised gardens (constituted by alternating layers of mud and decayed vegetable matter). This approach – which could be an exciting thing to experiment with and possibly contains elements in common with the methodology of *Hugelkultur* (a raised mound comprising various forms of vegetable matter with both quick and slow nutrient release, and differential exposure to light) – seems to have been invented by pre-imperial societies but then been taken over and generalised by the centralised state (Calnek, 1972; Redclift, 1987; Smith, 1996). Many forms of 'traditional' agriculture may thus represent a *compromise* between the two modes of organisation (centralist and emergent) to which we referred earlier. Although these two forms are in principle contradictory, in practice they found a modus vivendi which was *itself emergent and adaptive*. We could most likely make similar arguments about the West African empires, China, India, etc., which in contrast to a truncated and stagnant European feudalism, remained dynamic until undermined by colonial expansion. Such a compromise may indeed be a result of struggle from below; the sustainable paradigm is never merely technical, but has a political dimension as expressed by the agents of change which fight for it and, if this is true today, it may well always have been true. Wherever oppression exists, the movement for sustainability is a liberation struggle.

The most obvious way to present this theme is in terms of class struggle but there is a risk that this could be simplifying and reductionist. Therefore, two essential provisos must be made:

[1] Given the historical legacy of colonialism and slavery, and their prolongation in today's aggressive 'liberalisation', the oppressed peoples of the global South have a legitimate right to struggle at a *national* level. We therefore should not formulate the class issue in such a way as to deny national liberation. This issue is directly related to food sovereignty *in one of its dimensions*: the global

rulers, as an argument to sweep away impediments to their plunder, present state sovereignty in the South as outmoded, and this must be resisted.

[2] The movement of indigenous peoples, First Nations and tribal people connects us directly to the relationship between humanity and nature which prevailed before class society, and – just because of the back/forward dialectic described earlier – today constitutes also the most *advanced* force in the battle for a sustainable future, which is at the same time a struggle against genocide (physical and cultural). Any interpretation of class struggle which denies this fact would be Eurocentric and reactionary. Here again, we find a link with another of the dimensions of food sovereignty, which is in fact more important than sovereignty in some nationalistic sense: namely the demand to liberate some sphere (commons, neighbourhood etc.) within which to experiment with a re-alignment between humanity and nature.

The abiding need to challenge stagnant order

There is something profoundly important in 'deep tradition' and the indigenous principle, in bringing us closer not just to holism and equilibrium, but also to the progressive meaning of rift (*dis*equilibrium), an issue which will be crucial given the immensity of the task in tearing ourselves away from a dead paradigm.

Let us consider more closely what is meant by 'order' in a system. In the largest sense, organisation proceeds from the entire panarchy (Berkes and Folke, 2002). On the other hand, any particular phase of order is necessarily a simplification and, in this sense, 'a small set of critical processes create and maintain this self-organisation.' (Holling, 2001, p.391). This implies a 'site' or locus, wherein the determining norms of a given phase of order are reproduced, and which has in some sense a controlling role. All this is alright insofar as a system cannot be in total flux, but a problem arises when order rigidifies to the point of killing dynamism. In this case, the locus of determination will need to be challenged from somewhere which is not tied to maintaining it. This is one way we might interpret permaculture's recognition (c.f. Whitefield, 2004, pp.24–5; Holmgren, 1994) of the crucial role of marginal zones or 'edges', where a dominant order is less consolidated. This in turn suggests the issue of 'criticality', the frontier where '…you can move backwards and forwards between the two [order and chaos]….'

(King, 1996). 'Margins' here signify the *lisière*, the boundary where the region of cultivation *shades off into* the 'wild' forest, and we have full access to the latter's creativity.

If the above applies to physical ecologies, how do we translate it into social terms? The point is that there would likely arise a group with vested interests in reproducing a given order. Therefore, they would have to be challenged from some region of society where the norms are less consolidated. The socio-political implications of margins and zones of ambiguity – c.f. the link with Michel Foucault's ideas – are quite profound.

It is important to emphasise that the issue of avoiding stagnancy is never only an *internal* requirement of systems; on the contrary the issue is intrinsically environmental. This is because the only reason systems can *develop* – that is, become more complex and acquire self-organising faculties – is that they are 'open' (c.f. Prigogine and Stengers, 1984) to an external environment. And of course that environment is not merely passive, but has its own dynamism, which always poses fresh challenges to the systems which inhabit it. The demand for paradigm-shift therefore springs not just from internal causes but from the need to embrace environmental change (which is very much the case today).

Accordingly, for a non-Eurocentric historical materialism, the perspective of indigenous peoples ('tribal', First Nations etc.) must form a key point of reference. On the one hand, being the most marginalised by the current anti-ecological paradigm, they express the creative role of marginality. On the other hand, their tradition had a good understanding of the flexibility a society needs to respond to epochal environmental change. This is only really understandable if one takes a long-term view extending over many generations, which is exactly the indigenous viewpoint.

The ecofeminist perspective is similarly important here (c.f. Mies and Shiva, 1993), since women have been marginalised by all social systems, and more specifically agrarian ones, and can thus play a critical (in every sense) role in kick-starting change. However, to take the argument one step further, ecofeminism could itself be critiqued for taking on board the ascriptive characteristics of gender, and this is where the contribution of queer theory becomes important (Jackson, 1993; Clark, 2013). It challenges those categorisations and rigidities which restrict not only the human rights and personal development of groups within society but also the developmental potential of society as a whole, measured in its flexibility and adaptability. This again takes us back to the indigenous perspective, since we find in many traditional societies a culture which embraces such a disruption of norms. Thus, in Native American Navajo mythology (Williams, 1992), the people traverse a succession of sharply differentiated developmental phases, *which are in effect adjustments to changing environmental challenges and ecosystem discontinuities*, each of which requires profound changes in human culture and organisation [or paradigm-shift, in the terminology we have been employing]. Humanity is piloted through these transitions by the *nadle* (sometimes referred to in anthropological literature as 'berdaches' or two-spirit), i.e. people whose perspective is not confined to either gender, and therefore have the flexibility to comprehend transition at its profoundest level.

The above issue is central to visioning and transition, since in a situation like today where fundamental paradigm-shift is the only option, we need the ability to think radically and outside the confines of established norms.

8
Towards a new paradigm – practical guidelines

To sum up our discussion so far, the 'new' paradigm involves bringing together today's complexity-based (non-reductionist) science with a rediscovery of deep tradition. In this chapter we briefly discuss a few approaches which can concretise this.

The 'tame' and the 'wild'

In Chapter 7 we described a wrong – i.e. colonial/supremacist – way to determine oneself in relation to 'wild' nature. So is there a good way?

In fact, our demarcation from the 'wild' is not an abolition of it but a dialogue with how it spontaneously works. The farmed area posits itself as a negation of the wild but, unlike colonialism or modernisation, far from supposing superiority, we should respect the wild, welcome the diversity and services it provides and, above all, learn from it in designing our own systems.

There is a strange ambiguity in the notion of 'equilibrium', which the systems literature is sometimes too opaque about. An interesting pathway into this question is the issue of spontaneous plants ('weeds'). If the farm were indistinguishable from wildness, weeds would overtake it (Cabell and Oelofse, 2012). One way to conceptualise this is that any living entity has a boundary or 'skin' within which it maintains low entropy (c.f. Ho, 1998), and the boundaries of our plot are like this: if our farm was in 'equilibrium' with its environment in a thermodynamic sense, i.e. indistinguishable from it, it would cease to exist. For example, the nettle (*Urtica dioica*), while a very beneficial wild plant (serving as food, as an attractant for beneficial insects, as a source of fibre etc.)

might overwhelm our plot and, in fact, this would not be true wildness because, initially at least, it would lack diversity.

On the other hand, there does exist a meaning of equilibrium, or perhaps 'poise' would be a better term, which we definitely *do* want to have. This is part of the *criticality* we encountered in Chapter 6, a kind of 'fulcrum' where you can 'move backwards and forwards' (in Goodwin's words, quoted in King, 1996) between order and chaos; there's a connection between 'edges' in permaculture and the 'edge of chaos' in systems theory. We will return to the dialectics of equilibrium in Chapter 9, but the point for now is practical: the modernist negation of the 'wild' is to homogenise and simplify. The indigenous/sustainable demarcation is to create an edible forest which mimics the diversity produced by evolution of long historical time. We maintain this in a creative tension with the surrounding biodiversity, with which we're not in thermodynamic equilibrium, but we are in *harmony*.

Diversity here refers not just to diversity of species, but to plant *height*, and depth of rooting. In the practical application of this approach, these factors can be explored through intercropping and agroforestry.

In such techniques, there are different ways in which we can handle the relationship with spontaneous plants (weeds). In the classic Native American intercropping system, they are *suppressed* (Bilalis, et al., 2010): thus, tall maize plants deprive them of light, beans out-compete climbing weeds, and the broad leaves of squash cover the ground. The other pathway to reducing weeds is simply to expand the definition of edible plants to embrace many of them into the category of vegetables! In the author's allotment, we can include many self-seeded plants, which are either wild or self-seeding forms of cultivated strains, such as the wild hairy bittercress (*Cardamine hirsuta*), and land cress (*Barbarea verna*) which is a cultivated form which freely self-seeds. Because of the proximity of plots farmed by people originating from Jamaica, a semi-wild form of *Amaranthus viridis*, one of the sources of leaves known as callaloo, seeds itself freely, and we can introduce red orache (*Atriplex horensis rubra*) and then let it seed wherever. Rocket (*Eruca sativa*) is used in a similar way, along with the similar-tasting and 'wilder' form, *Diplotaxis tenuifolia*.

This takes us to an important point, the relationship between agriculture and gathering. In a rigid interpretation, gathering – which forms an important element in deep tradition – might be dismissed as less relevant to cultivation. In reality, however, the frontier between the two is much less strict than is sometimes thought. Turning again to the pre-Roman practices reconstructed in P.J. Reynolds' experiments in

England and Catalunya (Reynolds, 1985; Reynolds and Shaw, 1999), spontaneous plants – including Fat Hen (*Chenopodium album*) and wild oats (*Avena sterilis* and *Avena fatua*) – grew spontaneously in the field, greatly augmenting its nutritional output (and of course sparing the energy of weeding!). These systems were notable not just for their high food yield but for resilience: the forms of wheat which performed well, no matter how dire the conditions, were the more ancient (and closer to wild) forms, Emmer (*Triticum dicoccum*) and Einkorn (*Triticum monococcum*) (Reynolds and Shaw, 1999). The lesson is that – in contrast to modern approaches which unilaterally pursue yield volume by *narrowing the range of varieties* – the goals of yield and resilience can be fully harmonised, and must in fact be pursued in tandem; and for this, variety and variability are essential conditions.

The dialogue of human will with evolution

A key issue, again very relevant to how we relate to the 'wild' and to gathering, is the relationship of farming to evolution.

Partly, this means respect for *past* evolution: the plants on which we rely derive from strains whose immunities and robustness were honed over millennia. In modern strains, some characteristics have been 'bred out' so as to enhance food quality but we may still, when facing environmental challenges, need to re-access them. It is therefore crucial that 'wild and weedy' progenitors of cultivated crops be preserved (American Society of Agronomy, 2013). For instance, all apples in the world are probably descended from an original, *Malus sieversii*, found in Kazakhstan, where it is under threat (Fowler, 2014): we must retrieve it to access its evolved immunities which cultivated forms have lost. Thus, one of the methodologies which can contribute to the sustainability paradigm, Natural Systems Agriculture (NSA), 'is predicated on an evolutionary-ecological view of the world in which the essentials for sustainable living have been sorted out and tested in nature's ecosystems over millions of years...A primary feature of NSA is to sufficiently mimic the natural structure to be granted the function of its components.' (Jackson, 2002, p.1).

On the other hand, it would be simplistic just to see evolution as a purely spontaneous, 'wild' process, counterposed to cultivation. In reality, we have inherited a nature whose evolutionary processes have, again over millennia, been 'nudged' by humanity. The central principle is nicely formulated by Clement and colleagues: 'Plant domestication is a long-term process in which natural selection interacts with human selection driving changes that improve usefulness to humans and adaptations to domesticated landscapes' (Clement, et al., 2015, p.2). It is likely that farming originated from gathering, via 'in situ' management, in which beneficial plants were 'left standing' while others around were cleared (Landon, 2008), which would obviously, over time, influence how they evolve. This undermines any notion of an agricultural 'revolution' as a complete negation of gathering.

So, in this way, evolved species bear a long-term imprint of interaction with society. The modern peanut (*Arachis hypogaea*) is revealed as a hybrid between two divergently evolved and widely separated ancestral forms, which were subsequently brought back together by the migration of early American populations (Carmona, 2016). There is also much swapping of DNA in nature (remarkably, eight per cent of 'human' DNA is borrowed from viruses) (University of Michigan, 2016) and this, too, is something we have learned to work with, again in a kind of interaction between natural and human selection. Thus, a recently-identified case concerns the sweet potato (*Ipomoea batatas*). The root which we harvest is shown to be a product of bacterial genes which inserted themselves into the plant's DNA (Kyndt, et al., 2015) and, although this genetic insertion occurred spontaneously, what is significant is that the bacterial genes are present *only* in cultivated sweet potato strains, not in closely related wild ones. This is evidence that this naturally transgenic form was selected and propagated by humans (Kyndt, et al., 2015). Grafting, an ancient technique, has also been shown to involve a transfer of DNA (Le Page, 2016a). So tradition was nudging the genome in quite sophisticated ways.

In this way, evolution shades off into agroforestry, which probably arose through forest-dwellers' ongoing modification of their habitat. It seems they achieved this partly by understanding the positive role, within ecosystem development, of *disturbance*. Another relevant contemporary methodology, Regenerative Organic Agriculture, addresses the same issue in its aim to take 'advantage of the natural tendencies of ecosystems to regenerate when disturbed.' (Rodale Institute, 2014). Traditionally, a particular focus was the role of fire. In nature, by keeping a check on plants which would otherwise overwhelm others, fire maintains diversity and, when humans seek to suppress it, the system becomes homogenised (Li and Waller, 2015). Traditional approaches embraced fire, modifying the forest to increase the proportion of certain naturally occurring food-producing species. Thus, recent research correlating the composition of forests in the state of New York with the sites of precolonial Native American villages, reveals how their populations modified forests in ways which leave a lasting imprint today. Species which both yield nuts and are fire-tolerant occur in larger numbers than would be expected without intervention (Tulowiecki and Larsen, 2015). Similarly, while there is still debate on this, research on the Amazon suggests the extent to which, far from being pristine, it was quite intensively farmed prior to colonisation (Clement, et al., 2015). A recent study speaks of a 'complex mosaic of fire regimes [...] consistent with existing models of anthropogenic pyrodiversity...' (Liebmann, et al, 2016). It is important to note that interventions which modify forest composition do not necessarily lead to homogenisation. The result can be quite the contrary: thus, if we privilege fruit trees, this also has a positive impact on diversity of animal populations (Moore, et al., 2016).

While respecting the millennial legacies of evolution, we are also dealing with an *ongoing* process, since evolution, while partly very slow, can also be very quick. Some aspects are problematic for us, like the battle between antibiotics and bacterial resistance, and in a way this has its equivalent in farming: though we may use crop-rotation or sympathetic planting to confuse insect pests, the latter are evolutionarily selected to evade our ruses. Thus, 'When we disturb the ecology with our agricultural landscape, there are going to be consequences – even with the most ecologically benign approaches, such as crop rotation' (Seufferheld, 2015). We are therefore dealing with a dynamically changing natural order but can embrace this fact as part of our own evolutionary learning: just as evolution tests species, our farming systems are similarly tested and ameliorated. Seufferheld formulates this nicely: 'Understanding the interplay of ecology and evolution will allow us to design more sustainable agricultural practices...' (Seufferheld, 2015; c.f. also Chu, et al., 2015).

Seeds of oppression, seeds of hope

So what practical lessons can we draw from the above? An absolutely key issue for our food sustainability paradigm is plant breeding. In this respect, we may highlight two key requirements: (a) continuing to allow seeds to be tested against environmental challenge; and (b) farmer-based research. Today's corporate seed agendas (which we address further in Chapter 10, in the context of imperialism) stand in opposition to both these requirements.

There is a duality in today's science. On the one hand a progressive movement – with which we can unite – offers to embrace complexity and self-organisation, bring us back/forward to dialectics and reunite with indigenous principles. On the other hand, genetic modification (GM) has re-invigorated the mad dominationist dreams which still linger, as a kind of 'background radiation' from the Big Bang of nascent capitalism and the Death of Nature.

The mainstream approach typically creates genetically uniform cultivars with an appropriate combination of traits, and then continues reproducing them *with as little change as possible*: this is known as 'stability', and forms the basis of legislation such as in the EU, which tends to repress small seed companies who sell traditional strains. This is an example of the futile quest for predictability through homogenisation. Yet, paradoxically, corporate agendas also require *variety* of germplasm as a basis for their experiments. Hence the role attached to genebanks, most notably the Global Seed Vault ('doomsday vault') in Svalbard, Norway, a massive frozen repository sponsored by the Gates Foundation (CGIAR, 2013). These seeds are (a) cut off from the evolutionary process and (b) *taken from* communities without any interaction with them (c.f. Goldenberg, 2015). The two issues are linked because only through farmer-based research is it fully possible to explore a dialogue with evolution; otherwise we deprive humanity of the *process* whereby food systems should ceaselessly develop in their constant interaction with the environment. As Robert Henry puts it in critiquing the genebank approach, 'we effectively stop evolution when we do that. By keeping the plants in the wild, they will continue to evolve with climate change' (Henry, 2015, p.27).

A practical alternative is the approach known as evolutionary plant breeding, which encourages strains to *change themselves* as they are selected by environmental pressures. This methodology would critique the mainstream at several levels, of which the following are perhaps the most important:

[1] The issue of resilience: thus, '...the approach of creating uniform and genetically 'stable' cultivars that are deployed over large areas in monocultures is inappropriate for dealing with the current and predicted threats to agriculture. The response of these genetically uniform cultivars is not buffered against environmental fluctuations and novel stress factors when the direction and range of environmental changes are highly unpredictable.' (Döring, et al., 2011, p.1945).

[2] The issue of input: the only way in which conventional pedigree strains perform well is in conjunction with heavy use of synthetic inputs to raise fertility and control weeds, pests and diseases (Phillips and Wolfe, 2005, p.245).

[3] The issue of adaptability: as we saw in Chapter 5, micro-local specificity is the key to understanding soil ecosystems (c.f. Bardgett and van der Putten, 2014); thus, it is the very variability of non-standard strains which allows them to exploit particular niches. In an extremely interesting way, this argument also connects with the social argument for localism, in that 'by creating locally or regionally unique crops with their own "terroir", evolutionary breeding is in line with a re-connection between producer and consumer on a regional level…' (Döring, et al., 2011, p.1960).

Thus, in the same way that entropy stimulates complexity or conflict stimulates co-operation, stress stimulates resilience. Grassroots, farmer-based research has always worked with evolutionary defences and immunities, and a fascinating example of the directions this can take today is the work of French peasant Pascal Poot, in Lodève (Hérault), who left school aged 7 (Schepman, 2015; 1001 Gardens, 2015). His farm's soil is exceptionally poor and dry, yet his tomatoes are massively productive. He basically lets them strengthen themselves by battling harsh conditions, the key point being that this occurs *over successive generations* (he harvests seed as late as possible so that plants will have faced maximum stresses). It seems he doesn't *select* the seed, which would be the more normal way farmers 'nudge' evolution, but rather just reproduces the traditional strains, so what changes is not the genome itself, but gene expression.

University-based science is coming to think on similar lines, the starting point for this argument being that 'Plants can't get up and run away when they're being attacked by insects or harsh weather conditions. So they need mechanisms to rapidly respond to a stressful event – being eaten by a bug, for example – and then quickly transition back to 'normal' conditions when the stress level subsides' (North Carolina State University, 2015). Typically this information is conveyed by the hormone ethylene. It is the transcription factors – proteins that control gene expression – which are responsible for emergent behaviours, governing the way cells respond to stresses (for example, Lin, et al., 2015). This makes perfect sense if we step outside a linear determinism, since genes possess many isoforms (which may run to hundreds or even thousands) (c.f. Bolisetty, et al., 2015), and in this respect Dennis Noble interestingly employed an image of the 'music of life': rather than a one-way determinism from gene to organism, there are 'Loops of interacting downward and upward causation...' (Noble, 2006, p.51), controlling how genes are read. As if to confirm Noble's musical analogy, research now finds that cells alternately activate and de-activate the proteins governing gene expression through a rhythmic pulsing (Lin, et al., 2015) (other examples of plants' rhythmic sense will be discussed in Chapter 9). What Poot seems to demonstrate – and academic researchers are learning from him – is that some of these factors are heritable.

In all these ways, interaction with the environment is key. Most obviously, food systems must be resilient in *responding* to challenges – the adaptation issue. But, more profoundly, our food system can also *mitigate* environmental risk, and indeed has a responsibility to do so. This question forms the topic of our next chapter.

9
Regenerating the earth system, working with climate

Any viable future paradigm must meet mitigation and adaptation criteria. In fact this requirement should be seen not as a constraint, but rather as a responsibility – *and therefore freedom* – to think radically, outside the box. Although issues addressed in this chapter may seem at times technical, there is always a political undercurrent: this has to do with the relationship between *decoupling* development from emissions and *delinking* from capital accumulation circuits (as notably expressed in food value chains), as well as with a whole range of issues around citizen science, open-source, and generally the fact that transition must be a mass movement.

Plants as solar power stations

There is a rhythm in the earth system, whereby the carbon cycle is regulated by seasonal fluctuations in photosynthesis: NASA's Orbiting Carbon Observatory-2 (OCO-2) spotted a 'spring drawdown', 'a portrait of a dynamic, living planet. Between mid-May and mid-July 2015, OCO-2 saw a dramatic reduction in the abundance of atmospheric carbon dioxide across the northern hemisphere, as plants on land sprang to life and began rapidly absorbing carbon dioxide from the air to form new leaves, stems and roots.' (NASA Jet Propulsion Laboratory, 2015).

Photosynthesis uses solar energy to take carbon out of the atmosphere to build the plant and, in so doing, nature has evolved a solution to an extremely difficult problem. In quantum theory, a particle can behave as a wave, permitting it to explore multiple pathways simultaneously and, if only we could harness this, there would be unlimited potential. For example, quantum computers could explore all solutions to a problem at once. In practice, however, this is difficult to achieve. The problem is one we could perhaps represent as a contradiction between complexity and the ability to maintain quantum effects. Complexity enables a huge activity of self-organisation, 'messy' in a good sense, all of which involves heat and motion whose effect would tend to knock out quantum coherence. This is why most quantum experiments are conducted at extremely low temperatures, an example being today's D-Wave quantum computer which, cooled to a fraction above absolute zero (minus 273.15° C), is sometimes called the coldest spot in the universe! Plants face a similar problem to quantum computers (Institute of Photonic Sciences, 2013), but have solved this to near 100 per cent efficiency. When a photon of sunlight hits a magnesium atom in the chlorophyll, it dislodges an excited electron which is unstable, and the challenge is to get it to the reaction centre (the 'battery' where plants store energy) before the energy is lost. This is achieved by the particle exploring simultaneously all possible routes, and 'This wavelike characteristic of the energy transfer within the photosynthetic complex can explain its extreme efficiency, in that it allows the complexes to sample vast areas of phase space to find the most efficient path' (Engel, et al., 2007, p.782). However, it needs to maintain coherence while negotiating the 'chlorophyll forest' and this is done through a kind of rhythm internal to the plant (which has been detected in spinach for example): a 'beating' whereby coherence is maintained in a series of pulses on a scale of trillionths of a second (Al-Khalili and McFadden, 2014).

So in this sense plants are the most efficient solar power stations imaginable, and growing food can be seen as an important part of solar transition.

The role of feedbacks in plant-climate interaction

Farming is related to earth-system regulation as both cause and effect: influenced *by* climate, and at the same time impacting upon it.

With any such two-way cause-and-effect relationship, we encounter what are known in systems jargon as feedbacks. 'Positive feedback', which in everyday speech may imply something good, in systems theory often has a threatening tone because it describes any process where the output is also an input and could cause a runaway loop: as in the screeching when a microphone picks up sound from its own speakers and feeds it back into the amplifier.

The worst positive feedback would be if melting polar ice reduces the earth's albedo (whiteness), thus reflecting away less solar heat and therefore further warming the earth, melting more ice and so on. Avoiding this tipping point (threshold) is the mitigation issue. On the other hand, with some regime-shifts (state-shifts) discussed in Chapter 4, thresholds have already passed and it is too late to stop them: this is the adaptation issue. Food and farming are central to both.

What complicates it is that *negative* feedbacks could counteract climate change to some extent. There are two ways this could happen:

[1] as temperatures rise with global warming, additional heat increases growth, thus absorbing carbon;
[2] since there is more CO_2 around, this could have a similar effect, since carbon is the stuff of plants. Such a development could be good for two reasons:

(a) negative feedback might be the earth's way of returning to a self-regulating balance;
(b) more specifically, since food supply benefits from lusher growth, a food productivity gain in temperate regions might outweigh a loss (to drought, for example) at the tropics.

Drawing on recent research, what we can say is that we should definitely not pin too much hope on [1]: temperature increase cuts both ways, reducing growth as much as stimulating it. With respect to [2] on the other hand, recent research (Lu, et al., 2016) and, more specifically, a major study drawing on satellite data (Zhu, et al., 2016), suggests that CO_2 does indeed increase growth. Taking one particular case, simulations suggests that if Tibetan native grasslands are restored, their growth, stimulated by climate change, will mitigate the latter since the cooling effect of evapotranspiration outweighs loss of albedo (Shen, et al., 2015).

Thus (a) may be partly true in the sense that Gaia tries to function as a self-healing system, and this should be an incentive for us to make greater efforts to keep our side of the bargain. However, it is crucial that we don't rely on (b), i.e. some hypothetical climate-induced stimulus to food production. It has already been established that, following an initial increase of yield, this has tailed off and declined (Lobell and Field, 2007). Long-term predictions further emphasise the simple fact that, even if warmth increases at temperate latitudes, light does not! (Mora, et al., 2015). Furthermore, in the case of China, pollution (itself partly resulting from soil erosion) has hampered photosynthesis (Lin Changgui, et al., 2015), which would have the effect of reducing crop yields. The Intergovernmental Panel on Climate Change is therefore categorical: 'Based on many studies covering a wide range of regions and crops, negative impacts of climate change on crop yields have been more common than positive impacts (high confidence)' (IPCC, 2014, p.7). To this we can add a remarkable recent finding: increased growth may actually be accompanied by loss of *quality*, since plants respond to higher CO_2 by building proportionally more carbohydrate relative to protein, thus accentuating twin problems of obesity and nutrient deficiency (Ziska, et al., 2016).

While it remains true that anything green should absorb carbon – which is also one argument for greening the city – in reality it is not quite that simple because, in fact, the *way* we grow things is decisive and, if we do it wrong, greenhouse gas (GHG) emission from depleted soils will more than cancel out the absorption effect. A key reason is the bad interaction between nitrogen and carbon in the mainstream farming paradigm (Zhang, et al., 2013) and, according to latest research, if we include in our calculations methane (CH_4) and nitrous oxide (N_2O) as well as CO_2, a net GHG emission from various human land-uses is revealed (Tian, et al., 2016). This argument takes us yet again to the qualitative issue: the whole question is not how *much* we grow, but *how* we grow.

To address this issue of quality, we must understand the critical role played by soil ecosystems, both aboveground and belowground. It seems that, in the multi-loop linkage entwining biodiversity, farming and climate, a key element is how plant residues are consumed. Thus, the good (negative) feedback of increased warmth/CO_2 stimulating plant growth tends to be neutralised by a bad (positive) feedback in the form of enhanced microbial decomposition of this very same growth (van Groenigen, et al., 2014). But, and this is crucial, this bad effect could in turn be negated by the grazing of invertebrates within the soil system, who gobble up vegetable matter *before* it has decomposed, there being an interesting analogy with the aboveground grazing by large animals in limiting warming-induced changes in arctic ecosystems (Crowther, et al., 2015). The issue, therefore, is for our farming and land-management practices to operate in harmony with these natural feedbacks and the ecosystems which convey them.

There is a kind of earth-system balance involved here but, to understand it more deeply, let us revisit the subtle dialectics of 'equilibrium'.

In a thermodynamic sense, the essence of life is to be *not* in equilibrium with your environment (Prigogine and Stengers, 1984). The simplest organism must exploit a kind of 'gradient' between itself and its surroundings, allowing it to extract energy (Le Page, 2016b) and, similarly, earth exists as a living planet by keeping itself *distinct from* its surroundings (space) and by extracting energy from the sun, which is later dissipated (with higher entropy) into space (c.f. Penrose, 2010). The whole point is the internal structures – i.e. the complex systems, *built out of* this energy-transfer – which keep earth distinct from an inhospitable thermodynamic equilibrium with space (i.e. death). Recent research speaks of earth as a battery, equipped with energy stocks – within which the store of living biomass is critical (Schramski, et al., 2015). So again we encounter a kind of balance or 'poise' (a fragile one), which must be maintained: that's the good side of equilibrium. The way to achieve this is to implement agroecological practices which maintain and stimulate the beneficial organisms (such as grazing invertebrates) and processes.

Alongside the living biomass, we can also fix carbon in the soil. Soil holds nearly three times as much carbon as vegetation and twice that of the atmosphere (Wang, et al., 2011), and there is scope to increase this carbon content. At the most simplistic level, we could say that this carbon is merely 'removed' (sequestered), which in itself would be good. However, we can take the argument a crucial step further, since carbon also raises fertility (Lal, 2004). This is where the systemic process really becomes interesting. A good kind of positive feedback can occur which takes the following form: carbon in soil → more growth → more carbon taken from the atmosphere and fixed in soil → more growth, etc. This would in turn open up win-win scenarios, whereby we simultaneously feed the world and mitigate climate crisis, building a new order fuelled by the entropy of the old.

Here again, mitigation is not a constraint but an opportunity. Instead of merely minimising *damage* wrought by food-related emissions (food miles, methane emission from cattle, etc. etc.), we can/must set our sights much higher: develop farming as a benign geo-engineering which actively sucks in carbon. Thus, '…carbon dioxide should be regarded not simply as a 'bad' that has to be stored in underground caverns out of harm's way, but that it can be turned into a good that can be used to enhance the wellbeing of the biosphere and humanity' (Girardet and Mendonça, 2009, p.52). If the 'cavern' option (carbon capture and storage) is risky since there is a strong chance it will leak (Penn State, 2016), fixing it in the soil is both reliable and an actual gain. In a recent survey of different CO_2 options, fixation in the soil comes out top (Pierce, 2016), and continuing research backs this (Paustian, et al., 2016). Our principle should therefore be: 'Organic farming can reverse the agriculture ecosystem from a carbon source to a carbon sink' (Science China Press, 2015).

Moreover, the majority (60–70 per cent) of carbon entering the soil can fall into the category known as *recalcitrant*, remaining stable for millennia, which is of course what mitigation requires, and moreover the deeper the carbon, the more stable it is. If we discover how to stimulate this, we will be finding our way back to the indigenous mindset of thinking long-term, escaping the short-term mentality of capital profit-cycles.

There exist several ways to achieve this and, just to give an idea (without being exhaustive), we can mention a few:

[1] Grazing herds. The roots of perennial grasses can draw carbon several metres below the surface. This therefore raises the issue of how managed grasslands can become a fundamental component of climate mitigation. The UN Food and Agriculture Organization (FAO) made a big stir with a publication, *Livestock's Long Shadow* (FAO, 2006), correctly highlighting the unsustainability of the current mainstream meat industry. However, this touched off an interesting debate exploring how – though a radically different approach – livestock could make a beneficial contribution. Within this discussion, a contribution by Simon Fairlie (Fairlie, 2010) had an impact in changing thinking (e.g. Monbiot, 2010). The key point is that grazing animals are central to natural ecosystems, and we can work with this faculty. One approach developed by Zimbabwean environmentalist Allan Savory, involving periods of short intensive grazing, has given rise to both critical and supportive studies (Joseph, et al., 2002; Sanjari, et al., 2008). At least the general principle seems sound: by constantly cropping – and manuring – perennial grasslands, herds activate a 'pump' drawing carbon into the lower reaches of the soil, where it is sequestered.

Other approaches could be complementary to this one, and in some cases be implemented directly in urban, as well as rural, farming.

[2] Dynamic accumulators. These are plants which have a very deep root system (perhaps up to three metres) and draw nutrients from the rocky layer beneath the soil, the most famous being Russian Comfrey (*Symphytum x uplandicum*) Bocking 14, to which we referred in Chapter 3. If we regard our plot as a closed system, then in a high intensity model we would deplete the soil. If, on the other hand, we open it up to the subsoil and lithosphere

below, we can replenish its fertility, which in this case is achieved through a foliar feed made from comfrey leaves which stimulates growth of food crops.
- [3] Rockdust. Naturally, the weathering of rock can absorb carbon, safely transforming it into bicarbonate (Taylor, et al., 2015), and this has been adapted artificially by pulverising exposed volcanic rock. The environmental entrepreneurs who commercialise this procedure promote it as a way of simulating 'Earth's natural remineralisation process – 90,000 years of glaciers grinding rocks to fertilise the next stage of evolution.' (SEER Centre, n.d.). The effect, by raising soil fertility, would be another way of kick-starting a carbon pump.
- [4] An approach, which in this case leads us directly back to indigenous experience: terra preta (dark earths).

The latter refers to the historic tradition of building recalcitrant carbon deposits in the soil by pre-colonial Native American civilisations (Roach, 2008). Dark-earth sites are so closely associated with these populations that they form one of the main archaeological indicators in locating their settlements (McMichael, et al., 2014), while even today it is possible to observe this practice in action (Schmidt, 2013). It involves smouldering organic waste, and mixing the resultant charcoal with the soil. Such deposits still provide a high fertility over 1,000 years after they were laid down, proving that there is a win-win solution to the twin goals of long-term sequestration and intensive, sustainable food productivity.

The challenge is to rescue this legacy and make it a key element in a new farming paradigm (McHenry, 2009). In its modern form, terra preta is commonly known as 'biochar' (Steiner, 2009). In its academic aspect, the biochar project – involving, as it does, learning from traditional societies while also understanding what was going on in physical and chemical terms – is necessarily interdisciplinary (University of Wageningen, 2014). But crucially, this is not merely academic: biochar is an international social movement, aimed at creating a simple, low-cost and decentralised technology for pyrolysis. The essential point is that this is intrinsically a commons, open-source technology (International Biochar Initiative, n.d.), continuously refined through citizen science. It unites, on the one hand, the wisdom of crowds as an efficient knowledge-producing mechanism (because it harnesses properties of emergence and self-organisation) and, on the other hand, the demand for democratisation of knowledge.

This reinforces the political dimensions addressed in Chapters 6 and 7. It would be too easy to say that the need for systems to be 'far from equilibrium' is just a technical requirement of thermodynamics (governing dissipative relationships with the external environment), while harmony and balance prevail internally. Such an argument is clearly nonsense: what we need is disruptive forces from regions of a system which are less tied to the ruling paradigm. Superficially, this appears merely *reactive* (i.e. an adaptation issue): Thirsk's research (Thirsk, 1997) shows how, in British history, the ruling order is periodically weakened by environmental threats to which it has no response, and this in turn frees up social forces from below to innovate in *solving* the threat. This is already very interesting but we can go further: as the terra preta issue shows, indigenous deep tradition was somehow aware that we *make* our environment, not just respond to it. Today, we can restore this historical thread. The open-source terra preta movement, going beyond mere adaptation into a benign (biomimicked) environment-building, is a sign that this is happening.

10
Food, imperialism and dependency

As we have seen throughout this enquiry, many constructive elements for a sustainable paradigm already exist. Nonetheless, something prevents them cohering into an ensemble where they might determine a new mode of production. The obstacle is partly the difficult leap of consciousness to a true paradigm-shift, and partly repression by the ruling order... more specifically the structural forms this has acquired over the past century, which is the theme of the present chapter. By understanding what we are up against, we may better understand why the change-over – however technical it sometimes appears – inevitably involves political radicalism.

The 'Green Revolution' in the structural logic of imperialism

To create a social science of imperialism was not easy, and what is often missed is how, in doing so, Lenin found himself obliged to anticipate general systems theory. His most intensive study of dialectics (Lenin, 1972 [1914–16]), in other words of the dialogue between nature and consciousness, was undertaken in the period when his book *Imperialism, the Highest Stage of Capitalism* was under preparation.

Dialectics draws upon nature to understand processes of change and development, and one of its key principles is to grasp contradiction within phenomena as the driver of change. In this chapter, we will encounter several such dualities within imperialism, which encapsulate its essence.

Imperialism is an era of transition, and indeed of *rift*, in the sense that it tears history apart by pulling in two directions. On the one hand it is highly *reactionary* (both in militarism and politics), acting to suppress creative initiative. On the other, it 'drags the capitalists, against their will and consciousness, into some sort of new social order...' (Lenin, 1939). Thus, through the course of this era, elements of a new order are at the same time emerging and being held back. If, therefore, today's situation may sometimes seem exasperatingly static, there could be a dynamism within this: where two conflicting forces temporarily neutralise each other, something could rapidly unblock the situation.

Imperialism has two closely linked facets: structural change within capitalism and dominance over the global South. The exploitation and resistance of the peoples of the South is always a central theme, and new structural forms of capitalism evolve in a two-way relation of cause and effect. Such forms include the rise of mega-corporations and speculative finance capital, which serve simultaneously as mechanisms of accumulation, and structures to smother resistance. Both the corporate and finance-capital aspects of imperialism are exemplified in the food system, a system which therefore cannot be changed without challenging them.

In Chapter 4, we saw how capitalism, and more specifically its twentieth/twenty-first century form (imperialism), has been punctuated by several phases or 'waves'. On the one hand, each such phase has its unique characteristics – specifically, industries and technologies – which mark it out. On the other hand, it imparts path-dependencies which seem to endure throughout successive phase-shifts.

Let us consider the chemical industry: we've discussed (Chapter 3) the chemical paradigm as a 'fix' for feeding the urban poor. However, only by placing it in the context of the corporate interests driving imperialism can we get the full picture. While the chemical industry typified imperialism in its early twentieth-century form, it also initiated an enduring path-dependency, beginning with fertilisers, and then bringing in pesticides and herbicides. If, during later accumulation regimes, other new industries/technologies arose to assume a leading role, most notably biotech, these were still inscribed within a similar logic.

The driving narrative can be illustrated if we consider one of the key reference-points for food imperialism, the Green Revolution (GR).

In the strict sense this refers to a programme – strongly developed in the 1960s – to promote hybridised 'high-yielding varieties' (HYVs) of rice and wheat. Key to understanding the GR is an extremely close interdependence between chemicals and seeds. As with genetically modified organisms (GMOs) later, HYVs were deliberately bred so that they would only function with high inputs of chemicals (fertiliser, pesticide, etc.) and machinery manufactured by the corporations which sponsored the GR (Glaeser, 1987). For example, HYVs were bred to 'tolerate' herbicides which kill off competing plants. And because F1 (first generation) hybrids from two parent strains do not reproduce true to type, Southern farmers would remain eternally dependent on the seed supplier. In the economic logic of imperialism, it is *profitable* to sell seeds, fertiliser and pesticide. In the political logic, this builds a web of power, holding individual farmers and whole countries in thrall. Traditional approaches (where you work in partnership with natural ecologies, where insects aiming to eat your crop meet their evolved natural predators, where the primary defence against disease is evolved immunities, where intercropping or succession helps us 'borrow' immunities from one plant to protect its neighbour, where spontaneous plants are either incorporated for their properties or out-competed by ground cover) are repudiated. Instead, you simply *wipe out everything*. And indeed, expunging diversity is practically affirmed as a virtue: only a few staples were tolerated, and only a single strain of each.

All these interdependencies of profit and politics were experimented and refined through the GR so, in this sense (again a case of path-dependencies), we can say the GR is alive today, and GM is an extension of it. In fact the corporate interests and institutions forged during that period are still active: the Consultative Group on International Agriculture Research (CGIAR), effectively run by the World Bank, still quietly co-ordinates global research agendas (Alston, et al., 2006, p.326–7).

This is an embarrassing reality for the ruling instances, who still don't quite know how to handle the GR's legacy. When the UN Food and Agriculure Organization (FAO) speaks of 'greening the Green Revolution' (FAO, 2011), it adopts a cringingly ambiguous formulation, which somehow implies reforming what is basically unreformable.

We can analyse this whole picture of simplification and homogenisation at two levels.

(a) At a rational level, it is a most efficient form of exploitation and dominance. What underpins it is a deep connection between the reductionist-linear approach to science and political/social power. If, *conceptually*, you simplify a system and its chains of cause and effect, then *politically* it is easy to rule. In this way, by connecting political ecology with imperialism theory, via our case study of food, we may bring out certain features which will enrich both.

(b) On the other hand, however much capitalism may appears rationalist (even conspiratorial), this is in the deepest sense – as Merchant (1980) again shows – mere camouflage for a non-rational, manic and phallocentric control-freakery...which imperialism fully inherited. Elsewhere (Biel, 2012), I have explored the notion of 'exterminism', a term coined by E.P. Thompson (Thompson, 1980) and developed in an interesting way by Mark Jones (Jones, 2001). Since we are emphasising not just techniques, but mentalities, it would be important to see this in the context of the Cold War: the US bombing of Vietnam, Cambodia and Laos; napalm and Agent Orange. Internally in the US, too, there is a whole landscape of images around 'lawns' and 'weeds' which symbolise the extirpation of communism, and more generally of dissent and diversity. At a conference of the US elite, a Congressman, citing the authority of the FBI, openly compared eco-activists to Al Qaeda: 'This is a weed that has come into the lawn and if you don't cut it out, it will spread.' (Quoted in Biel, 2015b, p.39). From herbicide to genocide, there is somehow a continuum: expunging diversity, expunging weeds, expunging dissent.

Neo-colonialism's harsh impact on the global South

If the web of power is strong enough, a transition could be engineered from the formal colonialism of early imperialism into a 'neo-colonialism', where Southern elites are vouchsafed their own flags and anthems but remain in thrall to the core. It cannot be overemphasised how important control over a country's food supply has been as a condition for this. Cold War warrior Henry Kissinger openly boasted of using 'food as a weapon' (Linear, 1985). Conversely, it is precisely the hollow 'sovereignty' of neo-colonialism which is today being critiqued from below by food sovereignty movements.

In the process of an engineered food dependency, a major role was played by discourses of 'development' and modernisation. These had two functions: smashing 'tradition' (i.e. the good side of tradition: localism, autonomous knowledge and farmer-based research); and propagating a model where the goal of development was wholly identified with industrialisation, leaving agriculture starved of investment.

Thus, policies urged in the 1950s by development theorists like Walt Rostow imaged traditional societies as 'backward' *precisely because* their people were able to rely on the bounty of fertile lands (Rostow, 1958, p.159); this allegedly made them lazy so they had no incentive to become entrepreneurs. However, if the 'old' rural order had to be expunged, no autonomous modernised agriculture was allowed to take its place: to escape 'backwardness', developing nations must industrialise *rapidly* (the phrase Rostow used was 'takeoff', implying some sense of escape velocity), which meant extorting, somehow, a massive surplus from the countryside to feed the urban population *even though investment was all flowing into industry*. The result could only be to perpetuate food dependence.

Although, in its quintessential form, this approach was a product of Western imperialism, the notion of squeezing farmers to invest in industrial growth found a certain basis in Soviet policy too (Amin, 1981) (in contradiction to an opposite approach of sustainable agriculture in the USSR, which we will discuss in Chapter 12), and notably proved seductive to populist nationalist regimes with some anti-imperialist pretentions – Egypt under Nasser being a classic case. Mao Zedong in China was one of very few to realise that such an approach would be disastrous for development, *including that of industry* (Mao, 1977 [1956], p.286). As Amin showed, in contrast to a theoretical closed-economy model where the proceeds from exploiting farmers would remain within the national economy, accumulation circuits are in reality global (Amin, 1974): any surplus squeezed from the Southern agricultural sector tends to flow to the core. I would say that many lessons of the dependency school still apply (Biel, 2000), and the global food chains, which impose such horrific exploitation on Southern rural dwellers (Patel, 2008), can still be understood as expressions of accumulation on a world scale. It should be noted, too, that dependency implies its opposite: a delinked model (Amin 1986) in which national development serves in the first place that of agriculture (Amin 1980. p.144 ff.); here, the dependency school merits recognition as an antecedent of food sovereignty.

Since the promise of 'modernisation' was actually hollow, the resultant social formations readily subsumed the bad side of the tradition they claimed to reject. In pre-capitalist societies (feudal, or perhaps the better term is 'tributary' – Amin, 1980), there had been a kind of balance whereby wealthy rural elites had prescribed duties of patronage. In contrast, under neo-colonialism, as Baran points out, the exploitation of populations by their domestic agrarian rulers was '...freed of the mitigating constraints inherited from the feudal tradition' (Baran, 1958, p.76): in other words, the functional part of elite agrarian tradition was scrapped, leaving only the oppressive bit. This is why 'modernising' societies are often rooted in very primitive landholding structures, a point well made in the analysis of Indian society by the Naxalite revolutionaries of the 1960s (c.f. Bannerjee, 1984), and which has surely retained its relevance today.

An imperialism of resource flows, and how to fight it

For a still deeper perspective on exploitation, including its neo-colonial form, we should now consider resource flows.

As we argued earlier, one way to analyse a system is through its inputs and outputs. In urban/industrial society, linear flows replace loops (de Rosnay, 1979), inputs are thoughtlessly degraded, and excessive waste ejected. In a thermodynamic sense, we can represent the inflow as low entropy or 'exergy' (Hornborg, 2001), which turns into entropy when used up.

From this angle, we might approach the food system by examining only what flows into and out of it, leaving the mode of cultivation itself as a black box. Here, political ecology would consider how such flows are *controlled* and, on this topic, Malcolm Caldwell (1931–78) made crucial contributions:

[1] in his notion of 'protein imperialism' he showed how the meat industry in the core exists only on the basis of global flows of nutrients (Caldwell, 1977), thus providing a model for other exploitative flows;
[2] he showed how these global flows relate to the entropy issue, i.e. the degradation of energy/matter from a differentiated and 'available' form (where they constitute a resource) into a form where they become polluting waste (Caldwell, n.d.). In other words, we must see entropy and social exploitation as linked.

The deduction might be (still regarding the farming model itself as a 'black box') simply to liberate the food system from such exploitative flows. This would be one line of argument in favour of localism.

The above level of analysis, although somewhat helpful, is only partial. Caldwell's weakness was to remain subject to a chemical-reductionist view of agriculture which magnifies the role of inputs, notably of nitrogen, with the result that his argument has at times a pessimistic and Malthusian tone. This results from a one-sided reading of systems theory which overstresses thermodynamic flows at the expense of complexity. In reality, the whole point is what happens inside the 'black box': the magic ingredient which both keeps entropy low, and maintains the self-modifying faculty to embrace rift, is complexity. As we have argued, flows of energy into the system tend to be *negatively* rather than positively related to the effectiveness of a farming methodology, inasmuch as the more you subject the soil to *work*, the more you weaken complexity (by damaging soil structure, organisms, fungal networks, etc.). It follows that food sovereignty and agroecology must be complementary: it's not enough merely to delink the farming system from exploitative flows without also revolutionising cultivation *itself*, in order to rebuild complexity.

A good example of a technique which builds complexity is intercropping, whereby we imitate the multi-layered forest, including a canopy, climbers and ground cover plants, the most famous example being the Native American system incorporating maize, beans and squash (Landon, 2008). However, if we pursue this example, it suddenly becomes clear that what, at first sight, appears merely an issue of farming technique is really indissociable from social struggle, in this case a hidden history of South-South and South-North knowledge transfer. Thus, from Jack D. Forbes' remarkable research, we learn how native American crops like solanum, maize and curcubits were introduced to Africa independently of the colonialists, through a close interaction between African and native American peoples as they fought to survive the dual holocaust of the sixteenth century: colonisation of the Americas and the slave trade (Forbes, 1993). Food was central to surviving colonial/imperial genocide.

More recently, the struggle against colonialism and neo-colonialism remains similarly inseparable from a restoration of sustainability within farming. Thus the great African leader and martyr Thomas Sankara (1949–87) from Burkina Faso critiqued the food issue both as a material basis of dependency (c.f. Shuffield, 2006), and as a paradigm to understand – and therefore to fight – exploitation in a more general sense. Sankara was arguably the first statesman to link the political struggle (for land/food, against neo-colonialism) with explicit support for agroecology, c.f. his encouragement of agroecological projects conducted by Pierre Rabhi, which still continue (Terre et Humanisme, 2014). The orientation of Rabhi's work seems to be very much South→North and South→South: *not* about 'introducing' agroecology from outside, but rather enriching it, learning from indigenous techniques, which in practice *are* agroecology even if they do not use the name.

Trade specialisation and the rise of globalism

The notion of free trade was proposed quite early in capitalist history, at the beginning of the nineteenth century, by David Ricardo. The justification was international co-operation in place of nationalist competition, which seemed to make sense. However, there are too many crucial issues, notably ecological issues, which the theory sweeps aside. Its basis was the notion of 'comparative advantage', according to which each country should specialise in *only* the few products in which it could 'do best' (Ricardo, 1951). We cannot over-emphasise the importance of this point: under liberalism, *free trade is equivalent to specialisation*.

The most obvious ecological issue is to discount the impact of transport (plus refrigeration, etc.), hence the whole issue around food miles, but there is also something deeper.

The natural approach was always to cultivate a wide spread of crops, since, while any given year might be disastrous for some, this would not matter because it would be good for others. Every year is in some way 'extreme' and you may lose some crops completely: for example, the broad bean (*Vicia faba*) is prone to attack by a form of aphid, which is normally controlled by its natural predator, ladybirds (*Coccinellidae*). However, the disruption of seasons caused by climate change may lead to the latter breeding at the wrong time, in which case you lose the whole crop. Nevertheless, there will always be a bumper harvest of something else to compensate so, in that sense, there is no such thing as a 'bad year'. If you are specialised, on the contrary, both your livelihood as a farmer, and the food security of the consumer, will be jeopardised. Specialisation in agriculture is therefore antithetical to resilience. Although for the global South one could obviously say there is some comparative advantage for tropical crops, this argument is deceptive: the South's real 'advantage' under imperialism is cheap labour and lax environmental rules.

Given the exploitative potential, from an imperialist perspective the liberalisation of global trade seems a no-brainer.

Why, then, did it take so long to implement? The answer lies in the fact that a counter-trend also exists. One of imperialism's key dualities lies in the tension between its globalising face and its nationalistic/fascist/military face. Early imperialism, while highly internationalised at some level (notably investment), was also hyper-nationalist. In particular, wartime brought home the importance of food security as an offshoot of national security (thus an essentially militaristic definition). Accordingly, in the postwar/pre-neo-liberal phase (i.e. 1945 through to the 1980s), a strange situation prevailed: while the General Agreement on Tariffs and Trade (GATT) began tentatively to explore free trade *in industry*, in agriculture the capitalist powers actually became more nationalistic. The UK augmented its food self-sufficiency to a point where (by the early 1980s) *95 per cent* of indigenous-type food was locally grown (Barling, et al., 2008, p.11). That period in the history of food imperialism was extremely important, because it laid the foundation for where we are today. While colloquially we tend to call the global North 'industrialised' (which seems to imply the South is agricultural), in reality the powerhouse of agriculture is *also* in the North, while the South, owing to the impact of 'development' policies which throttled rural investment, must depend on imports either of food itself or of agricultural technology. Thus the nationalism of the core served to restrict and deny that of the periphery.

More specifically, the systemic power of the North is concretised under two aspects:

[1] The issue of staples (starchy crops that supply the majority of carbohydrates and are thus strategic for food security). Parts of the core where agribusiness productivity is extremely high become major staple food exporters (notably of wheat) to the South, often displacing indigenous staples (sorghum in India, maize in Mexico) in the process. Here, we again see how a system, by being simplified and homogenised, is easier to control.

It is precisely on the basis of being in control of the world food system that imperialism felt safe – under neo-liberalism and globalisation, from the early 1980s onward – to realise more fully the exploitative potential of 'free' trade *in industry*. While a tendency to import consumer manufactures from the South was always latent in imperialism – as shown in the predictions of Hobson (Hobson, 1902) – it took a long time to realise. I would argue that it required the North to build its food empire first.

[2] Global value chains in food. The point of value chains is to fragment productive processes, sub-contracting tasks to small firms for whom the core company has no responsibility; if they go bust, someone else will pick up the contract. This has spawned a whole terminology: 'flexibility', 'zero stocks', etc. (Biel, 2000). Initially, this system was experimented with in industry but, during the latter part of the 1980s and early 1990s, the value chain approach was extended to food. With the Uruguay Round of GATT (1986–94) and inauguration of the World Trade Organization (1995), agricultural trade was subsumed into global accumulation, along with the 'trading' of intellectual property rights, which were of key significance for food-related technologies. From a food-regimes standpoint, there was at the same time an effect in accentuating the North-South divide: when the limitations of productivism were revealed within the global North – its focus

solely on quantity had led to qualitative decline (Welch and Graham, 1999) – the intensive sector was internationalised (Marsden and Morley, 2014, p.8).

Once agricultural trade was globalised, this took to a whole new level the possibilities for controlling systems by homogenising them.

The effect was notably to promote an absurd expectation that there should be no seasonality in what we consume and that every crop must be available throughout the year. To take the case of asparagus, this can be grown perfectly well in England (as the author does), but only for six weeks per year, which is fine because that makes it special and there is a sense of expectation. Under globalisation, it is imported from Peru. Asparagus makes significant demands on water so, if there was any genuine comparative advantage, it would be from a country with plentiful water, but Peru is actually water-poor compared to the UK (Castanas, 2014). The legitimate aspiration is for people to have plenty of good-quality food every day; the insane aspiration is to have strawberries or asparagus 365 days a year. Yet the latter is what forms the basis of the flagship advertising campaign of the Tesco supermarket chain in Britain, with the slogan 'freshly clicked' (illustrated with graphics of asparagus and strawberries): you need only click your touchpad and they source the goods globally. The consumer has no connection with, or responsibility for, how this happens.

Homogenised systems are good for exploitation but bad for sustainability. Even now, neo-liberal economists shamelessly promote 'free trade' in food as a security against climate-induced scarcity (for example, Purdue University, 2016). The reality, however, is the opposite: any setup which is homogenised, de-localised and non-modular is vulnerable to shocks and system collapse; there is no security for any country, community, or city which depends on such a setup. Such a critique helps take our grasp of dependency beyond the point reached by the Dependency school: we now see it in terms of *systemic* vulnerabilities.

Agriculture and capital accumulation

The old farming paradigm was driven by *industrial* capitalism, in the following senses:

[1] *Politically*, the incentive was to feed urban proletarians enough to keep them docile.

[2] The *economic* incentive arises as follows: part of a worker's pay goes to replacing her/his subsistence, the remainder (surplus value, in Marx' terminology) being profit. Therefore, if you reduce the cost of subsistence (within which food obviously figures strongly), *profit in the industrial sector will rise.*

These arguments still apply, but a major change came with the crisis of the 1970s when conventional sectors dried up from an accumulation standpoint. Now, capitalism depends increasingly on agriculture as a means of accumulation in its own right.

We can interpret this conceptually in two ways:

(a) Rosa Luxemburg predicted, during the early twentieth-century imperialism debate (Luxemburg, 1913), that accumulation cannot reproduce itself out of nothing: it must always snatch, and commodify, new realms of existence, sucking each dry before clawing in the next (this is one reason why I argued that there is an 'entropy' intrinsic to capitalism – Biel, 2012). When neoliberalism came in, in the early 1980s (marking a qualitative increase of commodification at every level), it found much untapped potential in agriculture, as well as in farming-related 'intellectual property', notably biotechnology.
(b) As Marx revealed (Marx, 1954 [1887]), the competition of capitals creates a driving logic to replace labour by machines: in a large-scale, mechanised process, a handful of workers produce many goods, making the enterprise more competitive.

This latter tendency was initially realised in industry but has obvious implications for agriculture as well: today in parts of the global North perhaps 2–3 per cent of the population work in agriculture and, owing to the high level of technology, produce (unsustainably) vast volumes of food. Hence agriculture fully assumes the characteristic features of imperialism: concentration, agribusiness, factory farming.

Whereas the critique of productivism would address this same reality – the shift to agribusiness and mechanisation – from the standpoint of increasing the productivity *of land* (so as to feed more people), the Marxian argument adds the dimension of raising the productivity *of labour*. The difference is important, because it is by no means demonstrable that concentration actually *does* increase the productivity of land: small farms may in fact be at least as productive as agribusiness, if not more so (GRAIN, 2016, p.84). The fact that the productivity of labour increases is, however, indisputable. Using this logic – which humanity does not really want or need, but is forced by the structural dynamic of capitalism to follow – the result is not just to raise unemployment but, more specifically, to effect a depopulation of the countryside accompanied by a kind of urbanisation driven more by rural dispossession than by the promise of actual urban employment.

This argument is important for how we appraise the 'new paradigm' addressed in FAO/United Nations Conference on Trade and Development (UNCTAD) discourses. On the one hand, it calls for maintaining and indeed increasing *the productivity of land* ('sustainable intensification'). On the other hand, a renewed emphasis on small farms seems to imply a *decrease in the productivity of labour*: as rural livelihoods are rebuilt, farming will become more labour-intensive (as opposed to capital-intensive); quite possibly, too, a de-urbanising 'counter-exodus' will occur, whereby the proportion of rural population increases somewhat.

Does this model make sense, and can we afford to make farming more labour-intensive?

To answer this, we need to revisit our discussion of 'work'. The key point is that replacing human labour by technology means a *decrease* of efficiency, by destroying the free energy of self-organising soil systems (Chapters 5 and 7). Redressing this, a less technology-driven farming model would actually be more efficient. Of course we are not speaking of a neo-feudal future where serfs replace combine harvesters. The reason we do not need this is that today's mainstream paradigm is really an ultra-high-work system, in heavy energy deficit, each calorie of food requiring at least 10 calories of input (Glaeser and Phillips-Howard, 1987; Lott, 2011), which is, however, disguised by the use of fossil fuels. Potentially, therefore, the small-farm model makes sense but only with a simultaneous shift to low-work cultivation methods (such as 'do-nothing' farming – Fukuoka, 1978) inspired by 'deep tradition'.

We must also factor in the fact that the energy supplied by labour itself needs energy to feed it. This connects with a point highlighted by some environmental bloggers (e.g. Bluejay, 2013; Goodall, 2014), namely that if the calories consumed in physical exercise are replaced by food *produced under the current mainstream system*, it is more environmentally-friendly to put fossil fuels in your car, than to walk! The energy equation can be brought back into balance if we consume the low-input food we are producing (another argument for circularity and localism), while interestingly – as revealed by research among hunter-gatherers – an active lifestyle seems not to require more food

(Pontzer, et al., 2012) because the body adjusts. The solution, then, is to move back/forward to the situation which made Rostow apoplectic: people living from nature's bounty without working too much.

On this basis, we can say that the FAO/UNCTAD scenario of sustainable intensification plus small farms makes sense and is perfectly realisable *from an energy input/output angle*.

However, there are fundamental socio-political dimensions which the official discourse does not acknowledge. A knowledge-intensive, low-work system implies empowerment, a redistribution of power away from corporate intellectual property, and liberation from the dominance of global value chains. If these conditions are absent, the switch to small farms, which should in principle be progressive, could actually be just another form of exploitation. Let us explore the reasons for this.

Resisting the co-optation of small farmers in a new regime of imperialism

The possibility for a co-opted form of small enterprise was always latent in imperialism. It is implied by yet another of the dualities we keep encountering: on the one hand capitalism pushes towards modernity, monetary economy, the dominance of market relations, concentration (larger enterprises gobbling up small ones), and the replacement of labour by technology. *Superficially this appears very much the dominant trend*, highly typical of the imperialist phase. On the other hand, there was always a faculty for subsuming many kinds of more 'primitive' determinants. This is a major issue in the feminist critique of the household (Hartsock, 1983): the household was a unit inherited from patriarchal society ('bad tradition'), and subsumed under capitalism (Biel, 2000, p.133). Furthermore, sectors of the population marked out by ascribed gender and 'racial' determinants, or by informal (e.g. undocumented) status, are super-exploited in activities very often labour-intensive, self-employed and non-monetarised. A similar line of argument is seen in Dependency theory, according to which, 'insofar as primitive accumulation refers to accumulation on the basis of production with non-capitalist relations of production, it need not be prior to, but can also be contemporary with capitalist production and accumulation' (Frank, 1978, p.241).

In this, a tactic has always been to enlist the oppressed as agents in their own oppression and, here, the relationship with technology is interesting. Household appliances were advertised as liberatory, but were really just a way of anchoring the household in a new accumulation regime. There is an analogy with farming, because the chemical-intensive paradigm would be insecure if embodied only in corporations; it must also colonise the mind of small farmers. This was possible because the pre-modern system, *as peasants actually experienced it* (i.e. circumscribed by corrupted elites in collusion with colonialism), although formally organic, was the antithesis of a low-work deep tradition; on the contrary, it imposed backbreaking toil for low yields. Therefore, when modernism offered a false promise of liberation through a sanitised, homogenised world of chemicals and miracle seeds, a magical passport to predictable high yields free from vagaries of climate, a new prosperity, it is altogether understandable that many welcomed it.

The question is how to escape this situation today.

The kinds of paradigm-shift addressed by Kuhn (1970) were already a deeper issue (in world-view and modes of being) than typically envisaged by FAO-style 'paradigm-shift' discourses, but even then they took place in the minds of elite thinkers like Galileo. What we need now is something much deeper still, because it must come from below. It is a question of *conscientisation*: and whether in the work of Freire (1972), Biko (1978) or Fanon (1952), conscientisation is always about curing a colonisation of the mind. This is why the political side of the movement – food sovereignty – is inseparable from the physical cultivation methods (agroecology etc.). If you only have the politics (community autonomy, national sovereignty, etc.) without fundamentally changing the physical cultivation methods, it will be a failure and, conversely, to have only agroecology without the politics would be equally nonsensical.

In the absence of political radicalism, the 'new paradigm' might indeed be mere window-dressing for a new episode in the history of capitalism's super-exploitation of households and small producers. This is especially likely because, in its most recent phase, capitalism has indeed adapted to embrace principles of self-organisation and complexity, at least up to a point (Biel, 2012). With industrial value-chains, the whole issue is that these function *not by destroying small producers* – or even some elements of self-organisation amongst them, as in industrial clustering – but rather by corralling them into voluntary slavery. Foucault, in his work of the mid-1970s, prophetically described a power 'exercised through networks', and which 'functions only when it is part of a chain' (Foucault, 2003, p.29). In more recent specialist literature favourable to industrial organisation we find confirmation of this, in the fetishisation of concepts such as 'network capitalism' (defined as the culmination of three successive steps wherein governance has been exercised respectively through markets, hierarchies and networks) (e.g. von Tunzelmann, 2003, p.369).

Although the initial focus of such a re-positioning was industry, the theory behind it actually derived from small *peasant* production. A key notion is that of 'self-exploitation'. In elaborating this term, A.V. Chayanov (1888–1937) showed (Chayanov, 1966) how the peasant household organised its resources *internally* according to principles which were not capitalist (c.f. also Thorner, 1971). Parallel with this, there was also a way of exploiting what we could call a reverse alienation: earlier capitalism had caused a 'dis-embedding' – to employ a concept introduced in varying contexts by Karl and Michael Polanyi (Polanyi, K., 1944; Polanyi, M., 1962) – in other words, *a separation from real conditions, real place and real nature*. Now the new management literature recognises such separation to have been counter-productive, and advocates instead a re-discovery of *embeddedness* – in place, in local realities, but of course subordinated to global networks. The new management theories from the 1980s thus helped capitalism prolong its rule by parasitising non-capitalist modes of organisation which might in principle be those of a new phase of human society and, in fact, this is the worst form of capitalist exploitation. It should be obvious that all these methods would be eminently transposable to agricultural smallholders.

Accordingly, even *or perhaps especially* in a model where small farms were insulated to some extent from the circuits of capitalism in their *internal* operation – so long as the buyer-driven food chains (dominated by Northern conglomerates) retain *overall* systemic control – the setup would be exploitative. It is indeed more profitable for the monetarised, fully-capitalist sector to exploit units which internalise their reproduction costs, than it would be if everything was monetarised – an argument which would apply not just to rural small farms, but also to urban food-related initiatives, including community-based ones. In this sense, both small farmers in the rural 'new paradigm', and the new 'community' discourse of modified neo-liberalism in the city, could be complementary pathways to exploitation.

If we are aware of the dangers, they could be avoided, by for example small farms and local initiatives finding an alternative pole of attraction to shield them from exploitation by global chains. This is exactly why a militant food sovereignty movement is an indispensable ingredient, although it can be supplemented by community social movements, and in this sense the city has a crucial contribution to make, for example by setting up Community Supported Agriculture schemes. The point is to escape imperialism's perverse 'embedding', and move back/forward to a *meaningful* embedding within local cultures, knowledge systems and community networks.

Food sovereignty is, after all, merely a term currently attached to an emergent process, one which by definition is more than the sum of its parts. These parts include: land reform, indigenous struggles, food networks, seed exchange, community supported small farms, cooperatives, commons regimes in knowledge, localism, urban metabolism and many more. Such movements, generated by the reality of alienation and dispossession, are descendants of struggles going back to the origins of colonialism and class society, and the point now is to bring them together into an ensemble. The process is partly an objective one, common to self-organisation in all complex systems, and partly a subjective visioning of a better future. In any case, food sovereignty cannot fully be understood outside the context of the era within which it has arisen: that of imperialism.

11
Built systems, biomimicry and urban food-growing

We might sum up the future paradigm as 'working *with* and *like* nature'. We operate directly with nature, notably in farming and, at the same time, we apply similar principles to systems of our own making, tapping into the free energy of self-organising complex systems. Potentially, *mixed* built-natural systems could therefore encapsulate dis-alienation in an interesting way.

As we have seen, even agriculture at its most non-invasive (closest to deep tradition) is still modified, so in a sense 'built', by us. It could be argued, then, that a city is not *intrinsically* any more anti-nature than farming, and certainly not in comparison to today's mainstream chemical-based farming which needs healing every bit as much as the city does, probably more. Whether or not we accept the term 'anthropocene', this debate at least implies that we are living in a world extensively moulded by humanity: the human/built environment *exists*, we cannot wish it away, but we can/must transform it into something positive by reorganising it on the lines of natural systems.

In reality, biomimicry, self-organisation, evolution and symbiosis increasingly *do* form the paradigm in many areas of design, with the result that today's cutting-edge engineered systems are no longer antagonistic to nature as they once were. Indeed, in many respects, in areas like materials and design, the 'new paradigm' is already there: paradoxically, it is farming – which one might expect to be closest to nature – which lags behind!

The universality of structure

One basis for biomimicry is universality of pattern. Thus, '…the deepest ideas of math, if shown to be true, would almost invariably have consequences for physics and manifest themselves in nature in general.' (Yau, 2010, p.78). This role of pattern spans both life and non-living organisation: for example, bacteria arrange themselves in similar ways to the quantum arrangements adopted by electrons (Massachusetts Institute of Technology, 2016). A classic instance would be fractals, of which one striking example is the vegetable Romanesco (*Brassica oleracea var. botrytis*), which lays out its fractal pattern along a logarithmic spiral. The separation between art and science is also questioned, since art is sometimes the best way to come to grips with deeper truths. Thus, in cutting-edge research, amino-acid structures have been translated into music, because our ability to listen to them provides the richest way to grasp the 'intrinsic connections between the underlying structures…' (Giesa, et al., 2011, p.159).

In this way, a 'new paradigm for scientific inquiry' (Heylighen, 2008) breaks with the reductionist and mechanistic elements in Newtonian mechanics, in favour of qualities 'such as flexibility, autonomy and robustness, that traditional mechanistic systems lack. These qualities can all be seen as aspects of the process of self-organization that typifies complex systems: these systems spontaneously organize themselves so as to better cope with various internal and external perturbations and conflicts. This allows them to evolve and adapt to a constantly changing environment.' (Heylighen, 2008). Again, as we have seen with plants, evolution *tests* structures. The key is to be is adaptive and self-healing, hence robust.

Understanding the power of self-organisation unleashes astonishing possibilities. Recent research on solar energy storage explores an approach where materials 'self-assemble just by being placed in close proximity'. Its authors point out: 'We worked really hard to design something so we don't have to work very hard' (Science News, 2015). This is a beautiful statement which, although about something artificial, sums up perfectly how permaculture or Fukuoka regard farming: a lot of thinking goes into minimising work because the less we interfere, the more scope for self-organisation. Another nice formulation, by a group of robotics designers, is: 'In nature, complexity has a very low cost…' (University of California-San Diego, 2015).

Physical applications of biomimicry to the sustainable city

If we are to re-engineer the city towards sustainability, a key concept is 'urban metabolism'. Here, we again encounter the contradictory quality of equilibrium.

In nature, internal entropy is removed through a 'balance', whereby flows self-arrange in a way where the only linearity is inflow from the sun and dissipation into space. This faculty is lost in industrial-capitalist-urban systems. De Rosnay's diagrams reveal a striking insight (de Rosnay, 1979): *there is indeed a kind of regulation* within such systems, whereby they generate flows and even a rough-and-ready 'balance', but they can only achieve this at the expense of unsustainable linear flows *at the level of the system as a whole*: fossil fuels coming in, greenhouse gases/pollution going out. Our goal (c.f. Girardet and Mendonça, 2009) is to eliminate this. It seems that complexity is related to this goal *both as cause and effect*: a complex system can self-generate healthy internal flows while, conversely, by reducing linearity and hence entropy, we help complexity to grow...so this could become a benign feedback, which has implications at both physical and social levels.

Urban metabolism systems are nested: as well as occurring at whole-city level, self-organisation occurs within each constituent cluster, with the result that the overall structure gains added strength through modularity. One celebrated industrial symbiosis model, that of Kalundborg in Denmark, is seen as a case of self-organised spontaneous order which, in contrast to attempts to build eco-parks from scratch, exhibits greater robustness and resilience (Flint, 2013, p.117). On the one hand, issues around adaptive change (Holling, 2001; Holling, et al., 2002) make urban metabolisms behave like ecosystems. On the other hand, 'Our analysis suggests uniquely human social dynamics that transcend biology and redefine metaphors of urban "metabolism".' (Bettencourt, et al., 2007).

But examples of metabolism arising out of capitalism might – even if they reduce physical linearity – carry certain baggage, notably at a social level. Urban agriculture (UA) could help to redress this, which is one reason for its central importance within the city's re(self)engineering. It brings together several themes: the city *as* a garden; community gardens; wellbeing; meeting, conviviality and neighbourliness; diversity of experimentation, safeguarding free/open space from privatisation and enclosure; plurality against uniformity; common goods; experiencing nature etc. (c.f. Urban Gardening Manifest, 2014).

What has so far *held back* UA from fulfilling its potential in this respect is that it has been *either:*

(a) repressed/excluded;
(b) contained within parameters where it serves the ruling order.

In the global South – where UA would include many types of squatted, informally-occupied land and space – it has been mostly [a] which prevailed. It was despised and rejected by officialdom, at least till fairly recently, and it was relatively chaotic, which has the upside of being creative. In Britain, it was more [b]: through the allotment model, UA received official recognition but, in return, was circumscribed – by several parliamentary Acts spanning the period 1908–50 (UK Govt. 1998) – within a framework of 'food security', as part of national security. More recently there has been progress in breaking down these rigidities, permitting what we might call (in an allusion to evolution) a 'diversification'. Objectively UA *is* part of the metabolism but, by achieving recognition of this fact, we can take it to a new level. This opens up possibilities for a radical re-imagining of greening and food-growing.

At the time of writing, such a project is only embryonic, and much of it is still a vision. This is not of course a criticism, because vision is just what we need and, in fact, the *components* are already real, so our vision is mainly about the ensemble (Biel, 2013). As an aid, we could try to visualise the ensemble, for example digitally (Stuart, 2015), or we could, in the spirit of Eric Olin Wright's notion of 'real utopias' (Wright, 2010), extrapolate from trends which exist now, while remembering that, in our future vision, they'll flourish under new conditions. This will happen not least because they will have been honed and tested, in an evolutionary sense, by the challenges that they will have faced and overcome.

I earlier proposed a threefold analytical division for urban food-growing: the subsistence sector, the urban forest and the ultra-high productivity sector (Biel, 2013). The point was to register that there are several distinct reasons for urban farming, which can potentially interact. However, the distinction should not be rigid: for instance, the ultra-productive sector, though it contains elements of hi-tech, is not necessarily elitist, while its features of biomimicry make it part of the urban forest in some respects. The forest category is particularly interesting, in suggesting an interaction between the following themes:

[1] breaking down dualism between nature and the built;
[2] maximising the 'creative chaos' of self-organisation, in both physical systems and society;
[3] the 'wildness' required for biodiversity.

Where, in conventional plots, we mimic self-formed natural systems up to a point through intercropping, the urban forest takes this to the next level where farming and built environment cease being sharply separate (Wilson, 2009), with buildings becoming a bit like forests. Partly, the urban forest makes green space productive in food terms: for example, the trees we plant should yield fruit and nuts (Pinkerton and Hopkins, 2009), a process already underway in London (London Orchard Project, n.d.). In a more developed form, trees cohere as an edible urban forest which, once established, acquires its own self-maintaining ecology (Ettinger, 2012). In a social sense too, the process of creating these spaces is itself emergent, a spontaneous encroachment of growing spaces, as already foreshadowed by the squatted community of Bonnington Square, Vauxhall (Self-Help Housing, n.d.). The concept of forest is explicit in the Los Angeles community project L.A. Green Grounds (L.A. Green Grounds, n.d.), while the 'new ruralism' aspires to bring together smart growth, new urbanism and sustainable food/agriculture systems (SAGE, n.d.).

The whole essence of the 'forest' image is diversity, the positivity of the 'wild', getting back/forward to the indigenous principle of robust crops and 'nudged' nature. Hence, it will be important to embrace crops which, from the standpoint of the homogenised mainstream, are considered unconventional. The value of indigenous crops, which are nutritious and resistant, is at last being recognised (Cernansky, 2015), and urban botanical gardens could act as repositories and centres of education to promote these (Michelson, 2015). The author's experience would confirm the urban environment as ideal for experimenting with such crops, which can include native American crops like the tuberous plant oca (*Oxalis tuberosa*), or the achocha (*Cyclanthera pedata*, a climbing cucurbit distantly related to cucumber), as well as the Chinese artichoke or crosne (*Stachys affinis*) and a lettuce-related plant grown in China, celtuce (*Lactuca sativa var. angustana*). All this reveals huge scope for future innovation and creativity.

Integration of urban farming with the hi-tech sector

So how can/should this fit with the rest of the metabolism? Consistent with the rise of biomimicry in industrial design, a key issue could be the interaction between the hi-tech sector and the urban forest. Thus, the model of sustainable urban drainage systems (SUDS), in which planting is a key ingredient (Dover, 2015, p.40 ff.), is totally different from old-style urban water management: it introduces permeable pavements, vegetation and a subsurface of micro-organisms degrading pollutants (c.f. Dover, 2015, p.93 ff.) and is another way in which the city can be 'invaded' by green.

In particular, the new solar technology looks increasingly, and respectfully, at natural photosynthesis for inspiration. Progress is now being made along lines either inspired by the way plants use nanoscale structures to pull apart positive and negative charges (Science News, 2015), or drawing upon principles of symbiosis where, for example, 'artificial forests' of nanowires work together with bacteria, using solar power to sequester carbon and manufacture useful products in the process (Liu Chong, et al., 2015). These advances suggest great possibilities as a pattern for rooftops which symbiotically combine solar power and greening, using common principles of biomimicry.

Such an approach is already starting to be explored in a notion of 'biosolar roofs'. If we consider first the green-roof side of this model, we find a great case of spontaneous self-organisation: in place of the sedums which used to dominate (and homogenise) old-style green roofs, practitioners have now learned merely to lay a substrate, let nature take its course and watch the results (Gedge, 2013). What we find is that native plant species spontaneously appear, soon followed by rare birds, insects and arachnids (Kadas, 2006). Given that in a rural context biodiversity is heavily depleted by factory farming, monocropping and pesticides, the city actually becomes a sanctuary of biodiversity. If we now add the solar component, shade-loving wild plants spontaneously occupy niches beneath the raised and inclined solar panels in a manner reminiscent of agroforestry, while lowering ambient temperatures to increase the efficiency of solar photovoltaics (Gedge, 2013). Once again, it takes much knowledge to create systems where these things just 'happen' by themselves, but this is exactly what design communities are starting to acquire. The missing element in the biosolar model at the moment is, in the author's view, food growing. However, this could readily be incorporated.

Then we can add the social element of creating employment and education, something which again already exists as a developing practice. The hi-tech aspect of sustainable cities is not per se elitist or top-down, but has strong potential for community empowerment. A community-based rooftop solar power project already exists in an urban context in Brixton, South London (Rabagliati, 2014), and it is important that the paradigm for such experiments is the Social Work and Research Centre (commonly known as Barefoot College) in Tilonia, Rajasthan, India (Barefoot College, n.d.), which works with some of the most oppressed and marginalised rural women.

This in turn suggests an interesting notion: if, as we argued, the indigenous principle is about self-organisation and complexity, and cutting-edge design is about the same thing, can the two be brought together?

In practice, this *is* happening, and the back/forward dialectic has immense promise in urban contexts. The international Slow Food movement has a strong theme of 'Indigenous Voices' (Slow Food International, 2016), while it is interesting that cutting-edge, hi-tech, Sweden-based vertical-farming company Plantagon is chaired by veteran Native American activist Oren R. Lyons, Faithkeeper of the Turtle Clan, Onondaga Nation, part of the Haudenosaunee (Iroquois) confederacy (Plantagon, n.d.). In Canada, First Nations people are similarly a major driver in UA projects (Yves Cabannes, personal communication). Brafman and Beckstrom, in their argument for resilient systems where power is diffuse and modular, in fact reference the survival capacities of North American indigenous populations (Brafman and Beckstrom, 2006), specifically the Iroquois. This emphasises resilience, not just in the more superficial sense of readiness to bounce back after shocks, but in the profounder sense of readiness to embrace *dis*equilibrium as a vector for system change.

From the above, we can well envisage – using already verifiable components – a composite model comprising self-organised society, biomimicry in physical built systems, and an urban wing of agroecology. It would offer the robustness of self-engineered systems, while the indigenous component resists co-optation by the ruling order.

A critical view of technocentrism

While affirming the power of imagination, we should still ask a critical question about the viability of certain solutions. This question is not just technical, because it carries wider implications around the arrogance of technocentrism which, if not corrected, could keep us stuck in the old paradigm. A key case is the notion of growing food inside buildings. There is a few years of experience in this field (Despommier, 2013), and the world's first publicly-owned, open-data, crowdfunded, vertical farm research and education campus was recently established at Pasadena, Texas (Indoor Harvest Corp., 2015). Despite this, concrete successes so far are hardly enough to justify the grandiloquence of some claims. Critics – even those generally supportive of urban food growing – question the viability of indoor growing, notably on the grounds of energy cost (Cox, 2016).

I would say that the problem of energy cost is maybe not the main constraint, given extremely rapid progress in the efficiency of light emitting diodes (LEDs); and significant research *is* being conducted into LED application to food-growing (for example, Olvera-Gonzalez. et al., 2013). However, a deeper criticism of non-soil-based growing in general may need to address how far we can reproduce, *in an artificial growing medium,* the issues addressed in Chapter 4: natural complexity, in both the soil itself and surrounding ecosystem services.

This is a genuine question: the multi-layer aquaponic greenhouse system pioneered by Will Allen in Milwaukee, USA, does supply some reasonably convincing responses (Allen, 2013), in that it does constitute a spontaneously self-regulating system. Nevertheless, the weakness of 'visionaries' is often to sweep such awkward questions under the carpet. Thus, the Cairo-based rooftop aquaponics organisation, Shaduf, writes: 'as soil in natural conditions serves only as a reservoir for water and nutrients, water containing crucial minerals and adequate aeration let plants thrive on the rooftops without a grain of soil' (Climate Heroes, 2014). This statement is pure nonsense and goes counter to the whole notion of the soil as a complex system, in symbiosis with which plants have evolved.

Right now, some large-scale vertical projects appear viable commercially. Nevertheless, certain of their protagonists propagate the model with a weird line of reasoning which looks intuitively wrong. To cite a typical example (Shedlock, 2016), the argument is all about *eliminating risk and unpredictability*: proponents boast that there are no dodgy bacteria because sterility is monitored, the system is insulated from weather, etc. To cap it all, it is robotised so you do not have to worry about workers!

This kind of approach touches upon ideas signalled in Ulrich Beck's well-known critique of a 'risk society' (Beck, 1992). Beck himself framed his argument in what I would see as a deeply incorrect (i.e. Eurocentric and classist) way, by asserting that society has already *transcended* material want. In reality, want is still very much there (indeed increasing), but the point is, *risk-aversion is diametrically the wrong way to redress it*. On the contrary, the only way to surmount ecological crisis is to allow crops to strengthen themselves under testing conditions (including the messy world of bacteria). It is moreover not a virtue to exclude workers: the future universe of knowledge will come into being *through* the farmer, not by eliminating her/him.

The role of food-related networks

Despite these caveats, we do indeed witness a new ecosystem of initiatives, which recall a striking observation made by Holling in discussing points of system-change: 'reshuffling in the back loop of the cycle allows the possibility of new system configurations and opportunities utilizing the exotic and entirely novel entrants that had accumulated in earlier phases. The adaptive cycle opens transient windows of opportunity so that novel assortments can be generated.' (Holling, 2001, p.397). In the decade and a half since he wrote, so much has happened and many novel entrants now exist. The crisis of the old paradigm opens the window of opportunity for a new one, as an emergent assemblage of these components.

Clearly the urban metabolism cannot just represent *objective* self-organisation, independent of human will. What conveys and embodies the loops and flows are actually socio-institutional mechanisms: i.e. networks (these function in some sense as the social equivalent of the networks conveying information in the soil system). Here, the city can make a strong contribution to the strategic task of restructuring *rural* agriculture for sustainability. One key way this happens is through an interaction with the peri-urban area and, in this, networks play a big role. The best-known form is community supported agriculture (CSA), i.e. building stable links with peri-urban farmers, in order to offer predictability (in a good sense) to both consumers and producers.

Here again, we encounter the duality of risk: stability in an ecological sense is a false goal if we seek to attain it by artificially simplifying and homogenising systems, robbing them of their capacity to evolve in response to shocks. However, security in the sense of livelihoods – and hence the minimisation of risk to those livelihoods – is something we *should* always seek to attain. This seems to pose a dilemma for policy, but the solution will become clear if we understand the connection between the two definitions. The simplified and artificially stable systems, built in a futile attempt to banish risk from capitalism's urban-industrial future, are also very conducive to class dominance, thereby allowing privileged interests to manipulate the system's flows. Hence the risk, which is supposedly being eliminated from the system as a whole, is actually exported onto the oppressed and vulnerable (social classes, districts). It is futile to imagine we can improve the *distribution* of risk within such a system while leaving the system itself intact. Conversely (and this is where the argument becomes positive and optimistic), if we change the ecology of a system to make it more diverse, modular and robust – and hence *less artificially 'stable'* – this will also remove the power-nexus which reproduces insecurity at a livelihood level.

The best way to achieve this is through social movements. Applying such an approach to peri-urban farmers, the problem can be framed in the following way. The ecological argument to achieve resilience is diversity (in the way agroecology works with the soil system, in the range of crops and strains grown). Nevertheless, this will not automatically solve the problem in a livelihoods sense because, even in a good year, farmers suffer since there will be a glut, and supermarket chains can force prices down. Therefore, against the bad networks of capitalist value chains, we deploy the good ones of CSA, reducing farmers' insecurity through box schemes, which offer a guaranteed market. So, in this way, risk is magically dissipated (the main risk for consumers is having to consume seasonal produce, which is a good thing anyway!). An interesting way of concretising this, explored in Hackney Growing Communities in London (Growing Communities, n.d.), might be where UA focuses on those crops which must be consumed quickly – either because (like salads) they would wilt or, as in the case of peas, the sugars begin to convert to starch when they are picked – whereas other crops are sourced more from the peri-urban area.

And then, we may need to explore further steps, taking us beyond farmers' markets and CSA. Urban food-related network-formation is already beginning to generate its own literature (Cleveland, et al., 2014). It has been argued that the next step is *food hubs*, which can collect produce from many different producers and distribute it to many consumers. Through this process, farmers 'can plan together with the food hub to focus extra production in areas that minimize competition and maximize cooperation and collective benefits' (Wharton, 2016, p.144). There is a strong element of inclusivity. Although it is often assumed that people with low income will be forced to accept nutritionally worse diets, this is not necessarily the case: using the approaches we have discussed, good-quality food can be made available cheaply (Lifespan, 2016) while, similarly, farmers' markets do not just appeal to better-off people but can have a strongly positive impact on the less advantaged (Sadler, 2016). This is not just a building of food, but of society: studies suggest that such linkages carry a strong theme of moral values (University of Iowa, 2015).

Urban composting – the case for qualitative intensification

Supporting peri-urban farmers, distribution hubs, etc. – all this is vital. However, it still leaves the question of how meaningful a contribution can be made by food production *within* the city. We must always bear in mind where we began in Chapter 1: if the old paradigm is unsustainable, we must produce – in a new way – a *lot* of food. The reason for high-intensity UA is that, if the city can partially feed itself, this will buy crucial time to convert to wider food systems.

Some efforts at quantification which have been undertaken, particularly in the global North, suggest that the amount of food currently grown in urban agriculture is small. Thus the contribution of community food gardens is small when assessed for yield (though they can be important for other reasons) (Tomkins, 2014). A report on the campaign Growing a Million Meals for London revealed that 160 community food growing spaces produced 21 tonnes of food, estimated value £150,000, with a potential increase to about ten times as much (Sustain, 2014). This is billed as an 'achievement', but how many people would this really feed? Using a US estimate of 188 kg of vegetables per person per year (The Week, 2012), or alternatively the author's calculation of production on a home plot providing most of a person's fruit and vegetable needs (210 kg p.a.), a ballpark figure could be 200 kg. On this basis, the above-mentioned 'achievement' would impact the food security of only about 100 out of London's 8.5 million population.

So if conventional UA does not currently deliver, what can be done? For reasons just discussed, there are question-marks over the hi-tech sector, and although the latter undoubtedly supplies part of the solution, we should not be over-reliant on it. This suggests the goal of what we might call a 'qualitative intensification' of urban gardening.

In our earlier argument about rural agriculture we critiqued a narrow 'input-output' model which neglects the free energy of self-organisation available inside the 'black box' of farming methods themselves. The Malthusian error of Caldwell (1977) was to assume we cannot feed the global population if there are insufficient sources of nitrogen (N) (and we could make a similar argument about water for example).

Now, transposing this to the urban sector, there is a risk of making – on the same conceptual basis – an opposite error. Here, the confusing factor is not the paucity of inputs *but their abundance*: practically unlimited supplies of organic compostable waste and grey water are available through the urban metabolism.

Am I saying this is a bad thing? Not necessarily, but it is important that UA exercise a critical function with respect to the metabolism. While it is true that *some* metabolism will self-organise, it must be remembered that the high-entropy capitalist/industrial model is still dominant and, consequently, whatever loops and flows emerge are not *per se* guaranteed to be benign. Notably, UA might be treated as a sink or dumping-ground for whatever other sectors want to get rid of. We could then get lazy by relying on abundant inputs as an excuse for not correcting the farming system itself, and this would probably translate into entropy output.

Most obviously, we might input too much nitrogen (N). A project involving the author (*Closing the waste-energy-food loop – applying anaerobic digestate to urban agriculture*, University College London, 2015–16) showed that, while anaerobic digestion can produce plenty of high-quality fertiliser, the latter is high in N and, as we know, N pollution is one of today's main problems, which would presumably apply even if its source is organic. Crucially, the damage is not just in the form of the polluting effects of N runoff, but even more because of its knock-on effect on CO_2 emission (e.g. Zhang, et al., 2013). Now we come to a striking revelation of recent research: this is not just a rural problem; urban soils too emit very significant CO_2 (Decina, et al., 2016).

This strongly suggests that a major emphasis be placed on the *qualitative* character of land-management in cities, and particularly on converting land from emissions-source into carbon sink. This in turn implies a close examination of exactly how we farm in the city and, notably, what we use compost *for*.

The first point is that, in principle, composting is more about conserving soil structure than an input to raise fertility. The centrality of compost in this sense was established by Howard (1943), and has been carried forward in subsequent low-input methodologies (Dowding, 2007). Among practitioners, there is an aura of mystery around compost, which even has its own 'Da Vinci Code': a twelfth century manuscript of the Order of the Knights Templars discovered in an attic above a Spanish priory (Dailliez, 1981), which provides magical recipes for *composte de broussaille* gathered from the surrounding nature. In today's rural contexts large quantities of compostable material might be difficult to find, but in an urban context it is very easy. The key role of compost in this model is as a mulch, i.e. a layer protecting the soil and maintaining aeration, moisture and constant temperature (Dailliez, 1981, p.37).

Now we come to the issue of intensification. Once we have secured the minimum goal of maintaining soil structure and reversing greenhouse gas emission, it should then be possible to go one step further, into a high-intensity system where we maximise yield, for example, by mostly eliminating fallows and sowing another crop as soon as we have harvested the previous one. In this way, we might usefully absorb more compostable waste without causing runoff. Let us therefore consider a quantification. Literature on organic agriculture typically calls for a 40 mm mulch (Corbalan, 2005), which does not sound much. However it is surprisingly rare for authors to multiply this by the surface area to get a real idea of the volume required, so let us attempt this. Taking the traditional British allotment (250 m²), converted to a no-dig method with paths between beds and allowing for compost bins and sheds etc., our cultivable surface is about 150 m². Spread over 150 m² this gives a figure of 6 m³ required in a given year. It can be estimated that about half is internally generated from the plot. This gives a figure of 3 m³ per 250 m² of cultivable surface required from outside the plot's closed system, which in the author's practice, provides the basis for a truly intensive UA.

What precedents exist? We referred earlier (Chapter 3) to the French Physiocrat model, which could in a way be seen as a 'sustainable intensification', and the early nineteenth century saw an extremely interesting peri-urban experiment in the form of the *maraîchers* surrounding Paris: an ultra-intensive organic system, employing masses of compost and focussing solar energy through the use of cloches. It is, as always, important to understand the political subtext. As Jacobsohn importantly points out, the *maraîcher* project was a deliberate slap in the face to Malthusianism (Jacobsohn, 2016). Most obviously, the anti-Malthusian position is to demonstrate that human ingenuity *can* produce a lot of food, but there is more to it than that. To achieve this we must unleash the initiative of direct producers. For the utopian socialists, the way to prove Malthus wrong was the co-operative and associative principle. The Physiocrats failed because they did not challenge dispossession and, in fact, much of today's organic movement, permaculture, etc. are similarly blinkered in failing to unite with radical social causes. If our food-related networks can be linked to working-class associative traditions and indigenous traditions – *and if we can use these as a counterweight to accumulation and dispossession* – we can make it work!

The troubled legacy of modernism

The problem of a laissez-faire metabolism, which might reproduce the bad loops of capitalism, arises in both physical and social forms, and we must critique both in tandem: this is crucial to a meaningful political ecology, bridging nature and society. Hence the relationship of the new UA with notions of 'insurgent planning', activist scholars supporting social movements, and a re-definition of space. One example is a new approach to architecture which intrinsically incorporates food-growing, as in the AgroCité project in the cité of Colombes, suburb of Paris (Uncube, 2014). The issues around biomimicry and the universality of structure, with which we began this Chapter, are definitely not just technical, but intrinsically political.

In exploring this, an important insight is offered by the work of Alexander Kluge (Kluge, 2008). Kluge embarked on the realisation of a project which had once been initiated (and abandoned, because it seemed unrealisable) by Sergei Eisenstein: that of filming Marx' *Capital*. In a deep sense, we might view his work as an exploration of political ecology and a critical interrogation of biomimicry, conducted through art. Thus, describing Marx as 'the poet of our crisis' (Frankfurter Allgemeiner Zeitung, 2011), Kluge explores among other things the affinity between Marx and Ovid, the poet of metamorphoses. Here again, art can provide the best understanding of structure at a profound level.

On this topic, the legacy of modernism harbours an interesting ambiguity. The positive side is that modernism opened up respect for natural forms, and did have a core of political radicalism. We find both aspects in the work of Iannis Xenakis who was at the same time both composer and architect. His musical work *Metastasis*, closely inspired by his experience in the war as an anti-fascist partisan (c.f. Service, 2013), and which formed the inspiration for a notable building at the 1958 Brussels Expo on which he collaborated with Le Corbusier, draws also on the golden ratio inscribed by the same logarithmic spiral which we encountered in the vegetable Romanesco. The score of *Metastasis* (Xenakis, 1955) suggests a succession of phase transitions similar to Holling's model or to those (in the international political economy) set out in Figures 4.1 and 4.2 (Chapter 4). For the modernists, nature was key to healing the disjunction between form and function and, for Le Corbusier, furnished an inspiration for order (Dummet, 2007).

On the other hand, there was a rationalist distrust of *spontaneously* accreted cities, as they actually exist. While aspects of the 'green' were central to modernism, it was a very structured rather than spontaneous/ messy green. Even the garden city movement was in many ways strongly rationalist: Ebenezer Howard's model (Howard, 2012 [1902]), a very interesting attempt to re-integrate cities with their food system, is nevertheless rather the antithesis of an order self-formed out of chaos. In the London context, the Abercrombie Plan – a stunning vision of fingers of green connecting the centre to the Green Belt – also involved demolishing whole areas of the messy, accretive built city to make way for what looks like a rather un-natural and artificial green space.

This is the questionable side of rationalism. Accordingly, Austrian architect Friedensreich Hundertwasser (1928–2000) strongly critiqued modernism as an artificial imposition, not in any way truly emergent: 'When rust sets in on a razor blade, when a wall starts to get mouldy, when moss grows in a corner of a room, rounding its geometric angles, we should be glad because, together with the microbes and fungi, life is moving into the house and through this process we can more consciously become witnesses of architectural changes from which we have much to learn.' As cases of the good alternative to rationalism, he cited – alongside the work of Gaudí and *very few* other examples of architecture – workers' allotment garden-houses (Hundertwasser, 1964 [1958]). This is really about the creative facet of chaos, connecting with the arguments from Prigogine cited earlier.

Historically, the structure of many cities objectively *has* in fact self-assembled out of non-order, certainly in Britain and very much in the global South too. It is this which the bad side of modernism wanted to destroy. More specifically, the hostility to informal, messy and uncontrolled self-organisation was unsurprisingly manifested in hostility to UA, most notably in the global South. Thus, in a conventional narrative (e.g. Gore, 2008, p.55), UA, having already been repressed by colonial urban legislation, suffered still worse repression under modernising post-colonial regimes.

Indeed, to understand fully the modernist repression of UA, we have to place this in a wider context of demolitions, evictions, 'slum clearance' and social cleansing, all of which reflect a similar mind-set. The global South saw an atrocious legacy of destruction of informal settlements, in defiance of the right to the city. Even in London – if we take the case of a self-assembled and functional town centre like Brixton, South London – the intention in the 1960s and 1970s was simply to raze *everything* and start with a blank slate. A key element in this was the 'master plan', whose resonances are quite patriarchal and phallocratic.

The result would be to expunge complexity and cut short the ongoing adaptive process. There are crucial resonances here with our earlier argument about evolutionary plant breeding and in general the point that oversimplified systems are brittle and weak: if you do not embrace the creative side of chaos, you are left vulnerable to system-collapse higher up the panarchy. At the same time, whoever prescribes the recipe for a simplified system enjoys power over it: again, the intrinsic link between physical resilience and social justice.

This helps explain why struggles for the right to the city connect with urban food-growing at many levels. One of the most inspiring UA projects, which achieved a world-wide resonance, was the Garden of Eden, constructed behind 184 Forsyth Street, New York, by activist Adam Purple. The garden was destroyed in 1986 as part of an all-out attack on community gardens waged by Mayor Giuliani (for details see Reynolds, 2008, p.69; Carlsson, 2008, p.63). This is not to say that the spontaneous, emergent city is necessarily just because, after all, it emerged under capitalism; nevertheless, demolitions and 'slum clearance' have without question frequently occasioned still worse injustices.

Here, the work of Jane Jacobs (1916–2006) played an importantly positive role in a fightback against modernism's destructive face. Jacobs affirmed *both* an ecosystem approach to cities, and (in a socio-political sense) solidarity with popular struggles against neighbourhood destruction: it's precisely the link between ecology and politics which is key to her stance on self-organising complexity (c.f. Hirt and Zahm, 2012).

Jacobs' legacy led to a more holistic approach to the city, as an emergent, complex system in which built and ecosystemic elements interact. If we first recognise that this interaction is an objective reality anyway, we can then begin to operate in a new way which embraces and reinforces these faculties. On this basis, a new literature on urban systems (for example, Pinderhughes, 2004), could approach the city differently, as something which objectively *is* a kind of ecosystem where built and natural elements co-evolve. If we see cities 'as hybrid phenomena that emerge from the interactions between human and ecological processes' (Alberti, 2008, p.6), the issue becomes not the 'impact' of humans *upon* the environment but rather the emergent collective behaviours occurring through an interaction between the two. Since, importantly, complex systems do not follow a single trajectory to a single point of equilibrium, the goal of planning is not to impose a futile stability on dynamic systems, but rather to encourage resilience (c.f. Alberti, 2008, p.24). This perspective is obviously an urban-planning expression of the attitude to farming which we explored in earlier chapters, and therefore seems to supply the conceptual basis for a new, close integration of UA and urbanism.

Although all this is great, we must nevertheless be aware that the critique of modernism smuggled in some dangerous tendencies amongst its baggage. Notably, we must be careful not simply to laud spontaneous order in an unthinking way.

Perils of the neo-liberal city

The argument that spontaneous order equals best order is a neo-liberal one: exactly the argument for laissez-faire proposed by the high priest of neo-liberalism, Friedrich von Hayek (Hayek, 1964). The two linked flaws with this argument are:

(a) it makes abstraction of the overarching dominance of capitalism's circuits, and more broadly norms, which tends to channel any emergent social phenomena in a direction which reproduces these circuits/norms;
(b) it repudiates the visioning function – embodied in that form of emergence associated with consciousness, c.f. Chapter 6 – which is intrinsically human.

In this sense, the defeat of modernist rationalism could unleash new threats. A few examples can be given:

Firstly, while the spontaneous organic forms of the city have been vindicated, they are now vulnerable to place-marketing and gentrification. However much urban greening may play a good role in challenging binary town/country divisions, even a 'green' city can easily be co-opted as a market value. It is crucial, therefore, that the movement against gentrification and social/ethnic cleansing (c.f. Hancox, 2016) be a movement in defence of space, and an urban manifestation of the land struggle.

Secondly, the self-ordering of the city could reproduce inequalities rooted in the fabric of its structures. Thus, as Heynen points out, there is a bad metabolism through which today's city somehow reproduces the divisions of colonial city, as analysed by Fanon, into a well-fed white town and a hungry native town (Heynen, 2015). For this reason, urban political ecology, if it is to signify something real, must situate itself in the continuum of struggle against slavery and colonialism, and the issue of food deserts is one manifestation of this. African-American activists in the

US have pinpointed many of these issues: Will Allen strikingly places the contemporary food struggle within the context of slavery, its aftermath and legacy (Allen, 2013). So we cannot just worship emergent process which might be channelling exactly the metabolism which entrenches exploitation!

Thirdly, the conventional narrative of UA in cities of the global South (for example, Gore, 2008) rather misses the point about *why* the hold of modernism increased after independence. In reality, colonial powers had usually been quite clever at exploiting informality, and indeed imprisoning their subjects in a truncated limbo, stuck between a simulacrum of 'tradition' and an impossible aspiration for full admission to the capitalist core. This explains why post-colonial national and municipal authorities of the 1960s–1970s, only too relieved to have the oppressor off their backs, felt at last free to push modernisation. In this sense, neo-liberalism can be considered a kind of turning-back-the-clocks to the colonial era. As soon as the *global* rulers found themselves at last able – in the 1980s – to launch a revanchist dance of death on the grave of the modernist national project, it is natural that they would rediscover a 'tame' version of co-opted colonial informality. Although there are many positive aspects to the more enabling attitude to UA over the past few years, it is essential to remain aware of these co-optive dangers.

The answer to these dangers is again to emphasise the centrality of radical movements.

12
Autonomy, radicalism and the commons

Co-optation: the lingering threat

There is always, in food movements, the potential or vocation to be radical and subversive, break through dead equilibria, and open the way to a social re-ordering.

Today's generation of social movements to which food is central (Holt-Giménez and Patel, 2009) can therefore be placed within a long tradition of counter-systemic struggle. Thus, in the works of early nineteenth-century utopian socialism (utopianism being of special interest, given our concern with visioning), we find articulated a symbolic meaning of food beyond its material significance. In the work of Weitling, *humanity itself is ripening* (towards a stage where it can finally realise co-operative principles) while, at the same time, the physical harvest can only be maximised if we ourselves co-operate (Weitling, 1979 [1838], p.72 ff); one of the first communistic gatherings was a collective feast (Pillot, et al., 1979 [1840]). It is important to note that Marxism was conceived not as a denial of the utopians, but rather as a way of building on their work and taking it to the next level (Engels, 1970 [1880]; Geoghan, 2008). A further pivotal role was played by Kropotkin, who placed the food issue centrally within his discussion of revolution (Kropotkin, 1892). The English land and freedom movement of the 1970s proposed five interrelated tasks (c.f. Hobbs, 1976, p.136) – protection of the land, production of food, distribution of land, creating new human settlements, and providing for exchange learning of skills and knowledge. This is actually a brilliant formulation which has never been bettered, and forms a bridge linking centuries-old peasant and anti-colonial movements with today's food sovereignty/agroecology.

Taking all this together, we can say that food struggles encompass both the issues of immediate material livelihood, which all revolutions must address, and the big strategic issues going *beyond* immediate survival: dis-alienation, human rights and real democracy; all of which tend to converge in today's land and food struggles.

Nevertheless, alternative/organic food movements also have a serious vulnerability to co-optation. It is this duality that we need to address. While, on the one hand, radicals must connect with real, existing mass struggles on issues of significance to livelihoods (without which their politics would be meaningless), there is, on the other hand, always the risk of forgetting the strategic vision and dissipating radicalism into 'safe' channels.

A case in point is the history of home gardens in the nineteenth-century English Chartist movement. Food autonomy was an important issue for Chartists, leading many to turn to food production as an extension of their politics. In the early period around 1840, when Chartism was frankly insurrectionary (Peacock, 1969), there was a debate about this, with many leading activists critical of what they saw as side-tracking the movement away from its political goals. Later, under the influence of Feargus O'Connor, Chartism became strongly supportive of gardening activities (Willes, 2014, p.136). Does this signify co-optation or, alternatively, a tactical repositioning for a no-longer insurrectionary phase? These are the questions which can only be assessed in the concrete (not through any one-size-fits-all formula), and they will keep recurring in the historical dialectic. One example might be Argentina, where parts of the radical *piqueteros* movement of the early 2000s (c.f. Palomino, 2003) (we emphasise, *parts*, because it also subsists in factory occupations, alternative currencies etc.) have been channelled into food growing; is the effect to divert the movement from radicalism or, on the contrary, to root and embed it more profoundly? The answers must proceed from the specificities of each case, treating it as part of a discontinuous and 'lumpy' learning/conscientisation process leading eventually to the 'Hic Rhodus, hic salta' moment of radical system-change.

Is there something within sustainable farming which makes it vulnerable to co-optive manipulation? This question prompts us to delve deeper into some contradictions and ambiguities of its conceptual foundations.

Perverted discourses of 'community' and organics

Let us begin by interrogating general systems theory, which highlights similarities in the workings of all systems. It offers a great tool for identifying common features between society and ecology, and in this sense is fundamental to what we are attempting in this book. However, there are obvious risks – of which the feedback loop between social-Darwinism and Malthusianism already gave us some flavour – that dodgy readings of society can be transposed onto nature, and then transposed back again onto society to make them seem natural. Suppose we base our visioning of food futures on some 'harmonious' ideal of systems in equilibrium where there are no messy antagonisms. This would ignore the conflicts which necessarily and rightfully exist in exploitative societies whose populations suffer social and environmental injustices and would turn its back on the struggles of the oppressed, by which alone a new food system could come into being. From here, it is only a small step for the discourse to become a tool actively aiding the *repression* of these struggles.

We may begin by dissecting the notion of 'community'. As employed in ecological theory, for example by Odum (Odum, 1969), the strength of this term is to represent the diverse ensemble where all bits work together. By extension, this could offer an excellent metaphor for a co-operative reorganisation of society: with society running on similar principles to the ecology, everything would move back into harmony. This all sounds fine and, in a way, is close to what we are advocating in this book, which is all the more reason to be vigilant about how the argument could be perverted.

The problems are revealed by sociology's classic debate around the issue of community (*Gemeinschaft*) versus society (*Gesellschaft*). If we take 'society' as a representation of all that is modern and alienated, and community as the thing we need to get back to, such a discourse can easily be subsumed by reaction. In this sense, there is a kind of manipulative risk latent within the past/future dialectic.

To concretise this, we may take the case of Austrian biologist Ludwig von Bertalanffy (1901–72), who is revered as the founder of general systems theory, and his contributions should indeed be recognised. Nevertheless, von Bertalanffy, in the 1930s, adopted an indefensible attitude to the contemporaneous rise of Nazism (Pouvreau, 2009, p.61 ff).

The Nazis were peddling an eclectic mixture of pseudo-rationalism and mysticism. On the one hand, it was a social-Darwinism premised on extreme competition and Hobbesian *Führerprinzip*; on the other hand, some mock-historical notion of 'wholeness' and an 'organismic' interpretation of *Gemeinschaft*. In response, while von Bertalanffy critiqued the absurdities of the former, he did so only in order to uphold the latter: the organismic *Gemeinschaft* doctrine. In general, there was a whole land/nature theme within fascist ideology. We encounter this in the propaganda of Pétain's collaborationist regime in France, which centrally appealed to images of soil and land (Mirolo, 2011) (*la terre, elle, ne ment pas*). It was also during this period that Rudolf Steiner's biodynamic principles were gaining currency and this again is a complex issue. While aspects of biodynamics, notably the 'preparations' it employs, are being taken seriously in recent research on microbiology (e.g. Giannattasio, et al., 2013), there was nevertheless something in the mystique of harmony with land and soil which appealed to Nazis, causing Hitler – as McKay very interestingly describes (McKay, 2011) – to adopt biodynamics as the Reich's farming paradigm.

It is imperative to learn from this history, because co-optive dangers exist today, even if in a less obvious form.

The case of the Transition Towns (TT) movement is interesting in this context, particularly in relation to the urban focus of this book. It has a visioning methodology that not only features food-growing as a key component but was also in many ways inspired by permaculture methodology, which influenced TT founder Rob Hopkins in thinking about how society could learn from sustainable farming (Hopkins, 2015). Permaculture in turn picked up on Holling's and Odum's systemic view of issues like complexity, diversity and resilience. Accordingly, TT produced a 'forest model of society' (Hodgson and Hopkins, 2010) which looks quite like an idealised class hierarchy, with a nostalgic dose of feudalism thrown in. In this image, corporations dominate the forest canopy while social initiatives creep in the undergrowth, the implication being that everyone knows their place and touches their forelock in deference to the social order. Our reason for making this point is not to attack the Transition movement or permaculture, which both have some progressive potential, but they would need to be aware of the co-optive dangers before they could hope to realise that potential.

In addition to these 'old' co-optive themes, there are new ones more specific to current neo-liberal agendas. Thus, by transcending modernism (which, as we saw, inherently distrusted free self-organising from chaos), capitalism accesses a range of new co-optive options. If neo-liberal capitalism could harness and constrain the free energy of self-organisation, this could conserve the energies it might otherwise be forced (under Keynesianism, for example) to devote to running society...and thus allow it to offset the entropy of capitalism (Biel, 2012). In a manner anticipated by Foucault, a partially self-organising and decentralised system could run the system better than under modernism, and the 'community' theme could play a full part in this. Thus, community initiatives, including food-related ones, could easily be harnessed as a selling-point for gentrification and place-marketing (Slater, 2014). In London, right-wing populist Boris Johnson strongly promoted, during his mayoral tenure (2008–16), a programme of community food growing. This theme is closely related to the co-optability of resilience itself: a resilient food system is 'secure', in a sense which may be embraced by ruling security discourse (c.f. Neocleous, 2013) – a discourse that, post 9/11, encompasses anything and everything. In this way, the survivability of capitalism would be bolstered by the faculty of communities to survive somehow.

So it is vital to establish a line of demarcation from co-optive strategies of neo-liberalism. Where the latter embraces themes of 'community', resilience etc. in order to drag them away from radical class politics, we should assert that it is actually only *through* radical forces that we can arrive at a future where society and nature work on common principles. Concretely, we can aim to situate organics within a *socially critical* approach to general systems theory.

On this point, we can learn from systems theorist Edgar Morin (b. 1921), himself a veteran of anti-fascist resistance during the Second World War. Morin draws an important distinction between 'organicism', which instrumentally manipulates metaphors from nature, and 'organisation' in the sense of discovering common organising principles for human and natural systems (Morin, 2008, p.15). In fact, as Morin points out, the discourse of holism *may itself be reductionist*, it is just that it reduces things to the whole, rather than (as in conventional reductionism) to the parts; in place of this, he argues, we should speak of *confluence* (Morin, 1979). This argument closely connects with that of Levins and Lewontin, who uphold dialectics against 'the idealist holism which sees the whole as the embodiment of some ideal organizing principle...' (Levins and Lewontin, 1980, p.51). So maybe we can sense a kind of 'totalitarian' definition of holism underpinning the fascist co-optation of that notion. Similarly, co-optive approaches – fascist or neo-liberal – tend towards a discourse of 'no alternative', in contrast to the radical view of the future as open-ended and of crisis as opportunity. Significantly, Morin's recent work now converges with that of food/agriculture activists like Pierre Rabhi (a respected French Algerian agroecologist), as part of a project to respond to the crisis by visioning alternative solutions premised on altruism (Morin, et al., 2012).

The dominant discourse always tries to scare people away from the chaos which would ensue if the 'natural order' of privilege is shaken. In this context, the inbuilt conservatism of mainstream systems theory lies in its resistance to taking on board the advances made, beyond the Presocratics by Hegel, and then (beyond Hegel) by Marx (Shames, 1981). These advances might particularly emphasise the Hic Rhodus, hic salta moment of progressive rift.

Guerrilla gardening and the critique of the state

How, then, in practice, to escape the co-optive parody of organicism? This takes us to a question which has hovered right through our discussion so far: a socio-institutional equivalent for the panarchy which organises natural systems.

The centrality of this question may help explain why 'guerrilla' images are so prevalent in urban gardening: they makes direct appeal to self-organised struggles whose lack of a centre is a virtue because they are hard to repress. Thus, 'guerrilla urbanism' emphasises that the city is a human system and its emergent properties develop from its people: we cannot simply address self-organisation at a technical level without also embracing struggles for emancipation and environmental justice (Mares and Peña, 2010). At the same time, an explicit connection is made between the chaotic self-organisation of nature, and of society. Guerrilla gardening (Reynolds, 2008) seems to have an evolutionary capability to throw up new forms, one example being 'Guerrilla Grafters' who, in San Francisco, graft fruit-bearing branches onto ornamental trees (Zimet, 2012). It is a societal struggle conducted *through* the self-organising capacity of nature, as in guerrilla gardening's adaptation of Masanobu Fukuoka's seed-balls – whereby you toss randomly a variety of different seeds enrobed in clay and allow nature to choose where they are best suited to grow – as 'seed-bombs'. The whole of this approach is rooted in a subversive exploration of space: thus the notion of 'islands of unpredictability' (Carlsson, 2008) could be considered in a dual way, meaning both 'room' for experimentation, and an actual physical 'zone' where this happens.

So, in all these ways, by allowing unplanned and unstructured initiatives, we liberate the terrain for structure as an *emergent* property both of society and of nature.

This argument seems to tend in a very non-statist or anti-statist direction. Although, etymologically, anarchism suggests *absence* of rule, in reality it is probably quite similar to the 'panarchy' (Gunderson and Holling, 2002): there *is* 'an order', only the system itself (rather than any ruler) decides upon the order, and – importantly, since it is a dynamic order – how it develops. The strong historical link between anarchism and food issues, set in motion by Kropotkin (Kropotkin, 1892), was more recently developed in the work of anarchist theoretician/practitioner Colin Ward (1924–2010), whose commitment was strongly influenced by his study of food-related working-class self-organisation (Crouch and Ward, 1997). It is interesting that Ward, just like the Soviet dialecticians of the 1960s (c.f. Günther, 1964) (though Ward himself would not necessarily have wished for their company!), identified cybernetics as a key theme, interpreting this to mean the need for a society to self-organise *as a function of its complexity* (Ward, 1973).

Against this background, we might ask, why speak of 'food *sovereignty*'? After all, sovereignty is conventionally an attribute of the state and, in its classic form, (often called 'Westphalian' after the mid-seventeenth-century peace agreement which ended the Thirty Years' War) was a pure product of the European capitalist revolution. This implies dominance over a defined portion of the earth's surface and its resources, a kind of extension into international politics of the Baconian notion of dominating nature.

However, in reality, it is fair to say that food sovereignty as generally understood would distance itself from such a meaning. For example, in the Indian context, food sovereignty picks up many resonances from the Gandhian term *swaraj* to imply a sense of self-rule combining autonomy with curbing excess consumption. In parts of Latin America, such as Bolivia, the nation itself is redefined in a manner closer to indigenous notions of stewardship than to Baconian/Westphalian dominance. In general, then, food sovereignty is more about autonomy at a community level rather than at a national level, and is therefore perhaps not too different after all from an autonomist politics.

Based on the argument so far, it seems that a system which is not 'ruled' – in a conventional political sense – would be the social equivalent of a self-organised nature, and therefore the obvious basis to bring society and nature back together.

Although the above reasoning is neat, we must however remember we face an extremely serious task in transitioning to food sustainability, a task upon which – particularly given the interaction between farming and climate – it is no exaggeration to say that the future of humanity depends. Our attitude must therefore be responsible and not doctrinaire: we cannot simply dismiss a role for the state in the intermediate (transitional) phase before society moves more fully to self-organisation. The application to food/agriculture would explore the connections between:

(a) the notion of transition in socialist theory;
(b) the more specific meaning of a conversion period on the road to organic farming.

Concretely, you would need to escape the pull of current capitalist food circuits, organised at a world level (as recent trade agendas like TTIP illustrate all too well). If sustainable socio-ecological circuits are to re-establish themselves, it would be extremely helpful if they could be shielded from global ones.

Debating the history and continued relevance of socialism

One definition of socialism could follow from this: a transitional phase where state power is temporarily needed to shield a new society from being overthrown. Might we hypothesise that a socialist state could establish some supportive mutual respect for grassroots socio-agricultural practices, by analogy with the compromise forged (Chapter 7) by those pre-colonial empires (for example, in the Americas) which placed their authority behind a generalisation of sustainable practices which were initially trialled by popular experimentation?

It is true that the risk could be for something calling itself socialism to sink into a stagnancy which is no longer a transition to anything; or it could adopt a modernising tendency opposed to the re-integration with nature advocated by Marx, seeking to out-do capitalism on the terrain of productivism. Nevertheless, we should examine the experience concretely, if only to understand and learn from where it could go wrong.

Under Lenin, the Soviet Union promoted the brilliant geneticist Nikolai Ivanovich Vavilov (1887–1943) to lead a research programme which, premised on a deep respect for biodiversity and for the hands-on day-to-day experimentation of ordinary peasants, made the USSR the world leader in this field (Nabham, 2009).

This went tragically wrong later and, although many things went wrong under Stalin, this particular case is worth looking at more closely. The focal point of degeneration was the state-imposed dominance of the ideas of T.D. Lysenko. This is a complex and interesting question, because Lysenko was a peasant without formal training and some of the issues he raised remain relevant today:

[1] we should pay more attention to natural complementarities;
[2] practice suggests that, among food crops, certain acquired traits can be inherited, notably those which result from plants being exposed to challenging conditions.

It is worth recalling our earlier discussion of Pascal Poot: there is something about a peasant practitioner who is closer to traditional ways and able to see things which mainstream science misses.

Particularly in relation to [2], it is now clear that there is much subtlety in evolution – sometimes an adaptation occurs first and the mutation follows (as is probably the case with the first migrations of creatures onto land) or, in the case in question, events which trigger gene expression can influence succeeding generations. We can encompass this as an enrichment of natural selection without in any way contradicting it: as *New Scientist* rightly says, 'Evolution is true. But it is also a living, breathing idea that must not be allowed to ossify into a dogma of the kind that it has done so much to sweep away' (New Scientist, 2016, p.5).

Of course, the way science lives and breathes is only through vigorous debate and critical testing of theory. Where the Soviet experience turned to nightmare was that once Lysenko's ideas received official backing no-one dared challenge them and, in the absence of any grasp of the subtleties of gene expression, Darwinism was replaced by a full-scale Lamarckian model of inheritance of acquired characteristics, bolstered by fake experiments. Opponents were crushed and many (including Vavilov) killed, leading to a general collapse of science.

Drawing lessons from that tragic episode, obviously that was a perversion of socialism of which we must remain very wary. At the same time, we should remain equally aware that an instrumentalisation of agricultural science exists in a form imposed by *capitalism*, and people are getting killed all the time if they rebel against the Green Revolution or Monsanto. Indian farmer suicides numbered 12,360 in one year alone (2014) (Business Standard, 2015); a significant number of them can plausibly be considered Green Revolution-related. There could still be a role for a definition of socialism that:

(a) provides a shield against such imperialist corporate perversions of science;
(b) rigorously respects the highest standards of research; and
(c) pays full attention to the contribution of hands-on producers.

There is a postscript to this, relevant to the role of state power, which is the rise of organics in today's Russia. Recently, the Russian government approved an extremely radical strategy to restructure the whole agricultural system along organic lines (Case, 2015) and, although this is no longer socialist, it probably builds on aspects of the Soviet legacy while rejecting other bits. There was a whole interim narrative following the collapse of Lysenkoism which it would be interesting to research, notably the contribution of N.A. Krasil'nikov of the Soviet Academy of Sciences, Institute of Microbiology (Krasil'nikov, 1961 [1958]). Krasil'nikov promoted an organic method to which (amazingly, at the height of the Cold War) even the US looked for inspiration in addressing its dust-bowl problems. This may well have built on the work of N.I. Vavilov, and was of course also contemporary with the rediscovery of dialectics by E.V. Ilyenkov, which we discussed in Chapter 6. Although other aspects of Soviet agriculture were clearly not sustainable, after the Soviet system's collapse the weakening of the state made food security even worse (Ioffe, 2005). Accordingly, at the beginning of the 1990s, the remnant of the former Academy of Agricultural Science proposed a strategy to convert former state and collective farms to organics (Buys, 1993). So the recent pro-organic policy choice comes on the basis of quite a long and convoluted interaction between socialism, statism and organic transition, one which, (to re-appropriate Lenin's words), proceeds '...not directly, but by zigzags, not consciously but instinctively, not clearly perceiving its "final goal," but drawing closer to it gropingly, hesitatingly, and sometimes even with its back turned to it' (Lenin, 1972 [1908], p.378), but which gets there in the end.

This in turn provides a wider context within which to address the Cuban experience.

If we truly advocate feeding the world through small-scale, locally-organised (including, specifically, urban) agriculture, we would need convincing test cases. The two most obvious ones would be the 'Dig for Victory' campaign in Second World War Britain and the recent experience of Cuba. In both cases the state played a key role as initiator and facilitator, while the actual substance was decentralised, using small plots and local initiative. Yet the differences are fundamental. In Dig for Victory the actual production method – involving high inputs of a specially-conceived chemical fertiliser, National Growmore – was unsustainable. Even the name curiously embodies the fact that it was the antithesis of the no-till method (I would prefer 'No-dig for Victory'!). The Cuban model is in turn the antithesis of Dig for Victory, blending as it does the strengths of deep tradition with compatible inputs from modern science (such as biological pest control).

The Cuban experience had a big impact on urban food-related movements over recent years, notably through the film *Power of Community* (Arthur Morgan Institute, n.d.), which served as a major training tool for the Transition Towns movement. But *Power of Community* imposed a somewhat partial reading of the Cuban experience, emphasising the role of permaculture trainers at the expense of the Marxist dialectic. An alternative reading would emphasise that 'A major characteristic in the Marxist dialectical perspective is wholeness and the critique of reductionism. A recurrent theme in all of Cuban science is the breadth with which problems are approached and the willingness to span levels of organization' (Levins, 2004, p.7), an issue which relates directly to our key thesis, the readiness to embrace complexity. Specifically in relation to agriculture, it could be argued that Cuba took up the baton of the good side of the socialist tradition. One of the main things holding back organics globally is that R&D is dominated by corporate interests, whereas Cuba could channel huge research resources into organic research (Rosset, 1996). The key issue at stake is above all to reverse the loss of soil structure, and this is another issue which Cuba explicitly addressed (Gersper, et al., 1993). In this sense Cuba could be seen as a laboratory for the transition to sustainability, generating experiments of global significance which only anti-socialist bias currently prevents being more widely studied (Wright, J., 2012).

'Commons' as an abiding organisational solution

Whatever positive contribution the state may make to transition, this cannot replace the fundamental process of self-organisation, which must come from below.

There is good and bad in the realm of networking, and Deleuze and Guattari found a nice gardening metaphor to express this: rhizomes (Deleuze and Guattari, 1987, p.7). Rhizomes, they argue, include the best and the worst, potato [*Solanum tuberosum*] and couch grass [*Elymus repens*]. Therefore, fighting the bad networks (global food chains, intellectual property rules, etc.) must proceed reciprocally with cultivating good ones, and we need a principle to guide us. This is where the institution of commons becomes important.

Enclosure is an important notion in political ecology, as a representation of where it all started going wrong with the origins of capitalism and the Death of Nature. Enclosure signifies *both* an appropriation of land – in a sense where you were no longer bound by a duty of stewardship but could on the contrary do anything to it, chemically or technically – and *also* the destruction of an autonomous co-operative sphere of social self-rule which had survived even within an oppressive setup like feudalism.

However, commons proved resilient and, in fact, never really went away. There always subsisted a 'civic' or 'embedded' undercurrent within farming, working through reciprocity, and merely papered over by the dominant circuits (Lyson, 2004, pp.26–7). For all the market economy's totalitarian aspirations, there is a level of reality it cannot touch.

The fightback will involve a rediscovery and generalisation of commons, and in fact is already doing so. We can take this to include a diverse landscape of co-operative-type institutional projects (as revealed by research in which the author participated, *Mapping the Current Landscape of Food Co-operatives in London*, University College London, 2015–16), and it could in a broad sense encompass various institutional solutions to collective stewarding of resources, such as community land trusts (Davis J., 2010) or participatory budgeting (Cabannes and Delgado, 2015)...each of these being strongly applicable to food issues.

If indeed 'commoning' is the principle by which human beings have organised their existence on this earth for thousands of years (Federici and Caffentzis, 2013, p.2), there must be a reason why this particular institutional solution has been so persistent. We might seek this in relation to our earlier discussion of the universality of structure (Chapter 11), which could very well have an institutional as well as a physical dimension. In evolution, certain structures keep recurring (King, 1996) and, in the case of plants, evolution tends to explore a surprisingly well-defined region within the space of all possible combinations of traits (Díaz, et al., 2015). Similarly, we may argue, within an *institutional* space where anything is theoretically possible, this particular combination of traits known as commons keep recurring.

Commons signifies a certain attitude, both to nature, and to each other. Research has found altruism to be associated with a sense of 'awe' (Piff, et al., 2015), and we might interpret this to mean that the unifying principle is 'wonderment', as we contemplate a universe which – in both physical and social systems – requires co-operativity of its diverse components. We further see a connection in a notion of *care* (c.f. Davidson-Hunt and Berkes, 2003), which again would apply both to nature and to other people. The continuity with historic commons is more recently embodied in new, specifically urban, institutional forms which similarly bridge respect for nature and for social interaction. Thus, community gardens constitute '…microcosms of democracy, where people establish a sense of community and belonging to the land' (Carlsson, 2008, p.92), while the Atelier d'Architecture autogérée, while having an important food-growing component, also looks to community self-management in a broader sense (McGuirk, 2015).

As well as the persistent theme of land, there are issues like knowledge and seeds, which used to be open to everyone, but are increasingly exploited for private gain. Commons today can therefore be seen as a kind of node linking several new/old issues around land, knowledge and genetic resources.

Knowledge is especially interesting because, although an 'old' issue, it is also frequently seen as typifying the cutting edge of recent capitalism, where intangibles are traded more than physical goods. And it is widely acknowledged (even within the mainstream) that knowledge actually functions *better* as a commons (Bauwens, 2007), a point which somehow fleshes out Lenin's argument that imperialism 'drags the capitalists, against their will and consciousness, into some sort of new social order…' (Lenin, 1939). This has big implications for economics too: in contrast to a conventional economics premised on scarcity, information is abundant and potentially free (Mason, 2015). So on this reading, capitalism has made itself out of date: just as enclosure marked capitalism's irruption, the cyber-economy prepares its demise. This connects with Colin Ward's point that complexity, produced by the system's ongoing development, reaches a point where it can no longer be managed through simplification (c.f. Ward, 1973).

The crucial issue is that, while the knowledge economy is a creation of capitalism, the latter also *restricts* the potential of its creation: this is nowhere more evident than with agriculture-related issues (seeds, biotechnology), which are heavily restricted by corporate appropriation and patenting. Consequently, the full potential of knowledge commons can only be released by contestatory movements from below, and moreover ones which explore its re-connection with land/food issues. The Free/Libre Open Knowledge (FLOK) project, initially developed in Ecuador, is thus centrally concerned with food/agriculture, addressing 'the possibility and consequences of defining feeding as a commons...' (Vila-Viñas and Barandiaran, 2015).

However, while rightly stressing the 'beyond capitalism' theme, it is important not to get carried away with this argument to the point of neglecting the re-connection with indigenous principles: the latter have always been hostile to commodification (c.f. Taussig, 1980). In this context, it is particularly crucial not to overemphasise *information*, at the expense of wisdom. It is wisdom which really guides us in visioning futures (Bellinger, et al., n.d.), and as we have seen (Chapter 5), it is an intrinsic human trait that visioning be collaborative (Tomasello, et al., 2005) Strikingly, research now shows experimentally that wisdom is a product of the heart, not just of the mind (Grossmann, et al., 2016).

Faced with the subversive potential of commons, it is only to be expected that the ruling forces infiltrate commons debates from within, twisting the notion to serve their purposes. The ruling order needed first to break down the relationship of stewardship over resources practised by indigenous peoples, by transferring them into some realm of open access (D'Souza, n.d.); then they could be enclosed again, through privatisation. It would, however, be counter-productive to push this to a point where there no longer remained *any* dependent sphere of community initiatives upon which the ruling system can parasitise in order to meet the costs of social reproduction. Accordingly, mainstream institutional theory has discovered – notably through the work of Elinor Ostrom (Ostrom, 2005) – that commons can profitably occupy the region where 'excludability' is difficult (you cannot easily prevent other people accessing them) and 'subtractability' high (one person's usage diminishes that of others). Commons are therefore granted *recognition*, but at the expense of being contained within one segment or ecological niche of the institutional matrix, where the remainder of the capitalist economy can keep an eye on them. We might see this as analogous to the Transition movement's 'forest model of society' (Hodgson and Hopkins, 2010), where community initiatives creep in the undergrowth while big capital soaks up the sunlight. A niche institutional segment thus guarantees society its day-to-day minimum functions while gated cities of the privileged mine the benefits. This 'contained' commons is a kind of reversion to the feudal manorial economy, where serfs had their duck-ponds and sheep-runs but the lords still ran the show.

In response, the radical trend must do two things. Firstly, reject a *restriction* of commons to some 'acceptable' sphere. Of course, commons – as distinct from an open-access regime – may be legitimately focused on some *particular* and defined area or resource, with a particular community having access/stewardship/responsibility for it. Nevertheless, in the radical formulation associated with Gerrard Winstanley of the Diggers of 1649 (Winstanley, 1983 [1649]), which has proved a major inspiration for subsequent land/food struggles, commons implicitly and intrinsically embraces the whole earth. Secondly, insist on the *contestatory* traditions and values of the movement. In an important discussion document on the future of Community Food Projects, Ru Litherland points out that these 'can be seen as part of the rich tradition of self-help and mutual aid, alongside credit unions, breakfast clubs, co-operative societies and barn-raising, which enable individuals and communities to survive the inhuman effects of capitalism in the now, whilst constructing a set of steps which enable us to climb and view a vision of a juster world.' (Litherland, 2010, p.1–2). Applying this concretely, a typical programme of events from the Community Food Growers' Network in 2014 lists: a seed swap; projection of the documentary 'Raising Resistance' from Paraguayan farmers; a meeting on 'Pathways to Food Sovereignty'; support for Radical Housing Network's campaign 'London is Not for Sale'; a demonstration by the Land Workers' Alliance; a 'Peasants' Struggle' pub quiz; and an agroecology skill-share referencing sustainable agriculture in Tanzania (OrganicLea, 2014).

This again connects with the work of Colin Ward, of which it has been observed: 'Rather than sketching out utopian blueprints of a society without a state, [Ward] searched for empirical examples of everyday people organizing to solve their own problems. Once he started looking, he found that voluntary, non-authoritarian cooperation was everywhere.' (Walker, 2010).

A specifically human function is our ability to acquire 'information about the future' (Roederer, 2003, p.3) and, in this way, commons can be a *learning* tool, a way of accumulating practice in running society in a new way, one of constant self-critical testing, part of the process whereby revolutions overcome 'the inadequacies, weaknesses and paltrinesses of their first attempts' (Marx, 1969 [1852], p.401). This is very much the spirit of the Mexican Zapatistas, as they generate a set of practices, arrived at through trial and error and constantly analysed (EZLN, n.d.). There is a close analogy too with Lenin's point about trade unions acting as 'school' or 'apparatus' for the workers in learning to run production (Lenin, 1937 [1920], p.68). Agroecology is itself an alternative way of learning, an educational approach less elitist and pontificating, more akin to citizen science and action research and open to Foucault's ideas about critiquing power relations in the production of knowledge (Bell, M., 2011). It therefore naturally fits with those participatory research methodologies which draw on the work of Paulo Freire (Puttnam, et al., 2014). In all these ways, food initiatives contribute to the quest for a new order in which society and nature explore common principles of self-organisation.

This connects with the notion of autonomy, a key component of food sovereignty movements. The intrinsic link between food sovereignty and agroecology addresses a re-connection with nature, an issue essential to the Rights of Nature International Tribunal held in Paris to coincide with the COP 21 talks in 2015 (Global Alliance for the Rights of Nature, 2015). It is about making both nature and ourselves free from the unsustainable practices and global circuits which are destroying them. Thus in San Cristóbal de las Casas, Mexico, people held a Festival of the Free Tomato: free from social exploitation and agrotoxins...so the two kinds of freedom go together (Colectivo La Patria de Chiapas, 2013). Similarly, food transitions and societal transitions go together: a permaculture event in the same locality shows participants embraced by a geodesic dome (Instituto Permacultura Ná Lu'um, 2013). The geodesic was invented by Buckminster Fuller according to the principle of 'doing more with less' (Buckminster Fuller, 1982), which is a design principle exactly along the lines of the 'do-nothing' farming proposed by Fukuoka. And 'design' in permaculture means not an imposition of order *on* nature, but a conscious adopting of nature's own principles. In this sense, the technical side of agroecology is inseparable from the social and institutional way in which farming – and in a broader sense food networks, and in a still broader sense society as a whole – organises itself.

There is a duality within humanity. On the one hand we are capable of bringing collaboration and holism to the level of dialectical thought and a conscious futures visioning but, on the other hand, we have separated ourselves from nature and built structures – including, eminently, land/food systems – which exploit and degrade nature and ourselves. Winstanley, in seeking to articulate this duality, forged a remarkable conceptual vocabulary which, while in some ways anticipating Blake in its imagery, anticipates also the Enlightenment with its appeals to reason. Through this, he challenges the narrative through which the selfish and exploitative Esau, or Cain, persistently slays his brother:

> And thus Esau, the man of flesh which is covetousness and pride, hath killed Jacob, the spirit of meekness and righteous government in the light of reason, and rules over him: and so the earth, that was made a common treasury for all to live comfortably upon, is become through man's unrighteous actions one over another to be a place wherein one torments another'; '…the earth hath been enclosed and given to the elder brother Esau, or man of flesh, and hath been bought and sold from one to another; and Jacob, or the younger brother, that is to succeed or come forth next, who is the universal spreading power of righteousness that gives liberty to the whole creation, is made a servant. (Winstanley, 1983 [1649], p.79)

To overturn this injustice is the culmination of a big historical process, in which we are now called upon to participate. For all the special features of capitalism analysed in this book, the issue actually goes much deeper. This is notably the case with agrarian systems, where today's social movements for food sovereignty and land rights are a culmination of a secular history of rebellions by slaves, serfs, indigenous and colonised peoples, all those stigmatised and excluded through gender and 'racial' determinants, indentured workers, sharecroppers and in general everyone dispossessed, displaced and alienated from the land/earth. Launching a collective process of analysis of the current crisis, timed to take place on May 3, 'the day of planting, of fertility, of harvest, of seeds', the Zapatistas argue: 'theoretical reflection and critical thought have the same task as the sentinel. Whoever works on analytic thinking takes a shift as guard at the watchpost' (Galeano, 2015). It is a heavy responsibility to get this right and not allow ourselves to be distracted by partial and distorted observation. The reward of getting it right is the possibility of settling accounts with the oppressive legacy of history and moving forward, to a new regime in relation to food, land and the earth.

Bibliography

1001 Gardens, 2015. *Without water, he found out how to grow tomatoes.* [online] Available at: <http://www.1001gardens.org/2015/08/without-water-he-found-out-how-to-grow-tomatoes/> [Accessed 2.08.15]
Acton, L., 2011. *The allotment movement in North-East Greater London 1900–2010*. PhD Thesis. London: UCL.
Alberti, M., 2008. *Advances in urban ecology – integrating human and ecological processes in urban ecosystems.* New York: Springer Science.
Al-Khalili, J. and McFadden, J., 2014. *Life on the edge: the coming of age of quantum biology.* London: Bantam.
Allen, W., 2013. *The good food revolution.* New York: Gotham Books.
Alston, J.M., Dehmer, S. and Pardy, P.G., 2006. International initiatives in agricultural R&D – the changing fortunes of the CGIAR. In: P.G. Pardey, J.M. Alston, and R. Piggott, eds. *Agricultural R&D in the developing world: too little, too late?* Washington DC: International Food Policy Research Institute.
American Society of Agronomy, 2013. Protecting the weedy and wild kin of globally important crops. *ScienceDaily*, 1 October. [online] Available at: <www.sciencedaily.com/releases/2013/10/131001221215.htm> [Accessed 28.3.16]
Amin, S., 1974. *Accumulation on a world scale – a critique of the theory of underdevelopment*, two vols. New York: Monthly Review.
Amin, S., 1980. *Class and nation – historically and in the current crisis.* London: Heinemann.
Amin, S., 1981. *L'avenir du Maoïsme.* Paris: Editions du Minuit.
Amin, S., 1986. *La déconnection – pour sortir du système mondiale.* Paris: La Découverte.
Amundson, R. et al., 2015. Soil and human security in the 21st century. *Science*, vol. 348 no. 6235: 1261071 DOI: 10.1126/science.1261071
Armitage, S. et al., 2015. West African monsoon dynamics inferred from abrupt fluctuations of Lake Mega-Chad. *PNAS*, June. DOI: 10.1073/pnas.1417655112
Arriaga, F. et al., 2012. Soil erosion concerns after silage harvest. *New Horizons in Soil Science*, 12–03, Department of Soil Science, University of Wisconsin-Madison.
Arthur Morgan Institute, n.d. *The power of community – how Cuba survived peak oil.* Feature film. [online] Available at: <http://www.communitysolution.org/mediaandeducation/films/powerofcommunity/> [Accessed 1.8.16]
Associated Press, 2012. *Hundreds Of suicides in India linked to microfinance organizations.* 24 February [online] Available at: <http://www.businessinsider.com/hundreds-of-suicides-in-india-linked-to-microfinance-organizations-2012-2?IR=T> [Accessed 1.8.16]
Attwater, J. and Holliger, P., 2012. Origins of life: The cooperative gene. *Nature* 491(7422); 1 November): 48–9. Epub 17 October 2012.
Bannerjee, S., 1984. *India's simmering revolution.* 2nd revised edition. London: Zed Books.
Banwart, S., 2011. Save our soils. *Nature* 474: 151–152 (9 June). DOI: 10.1038/474151a
Baran, P., 1958. On the political economy of backwardness. In: A.N. Agarwala and S.P. Singh, eds. *The economics of underdevelopment.* Delhi: Oxford University Press.
Baranger, M., n.d. *Chaos, complexity, and entropy,* discussion paper, Center for Theoretical Physics, Laboratory for Nuclear Science and Department of Physics, Massachusetts Institute of Technology. [online] Available at: <http://www.necsi.org/projects/baranger/cce.pdf> [Accessed 3.4.15]

Bardgett, R.D. and van der Putten, W.H., 2014. Belowground biodiversity and ecosystem functioning. *Nature* 515 (27 November), 505–11. DOI: 10.1038/nature13855

Barefoot College, n.d. *Solar*. [online] Available at: <http://www.barefootcollege.org/solutions/solar-solutions/> [Accessed 11.6.15]

Barkun, M., 1968. *Law without sanctions – order in primitive societies and the world community*. New Haven: Yale University Press.

Barling, D., Sharpe, R. and Lang, T., 2008. *Towards a national sustainable food security policy – a project to map the policy interface between food security and sustainable food supply*. London: City University, Centre for Food Policy.

Barnaby, W., 2009. Do nations go to war over water? *Nature*, 458 (March 19): 282–3.

Barnosky, A.D. et al., 2012. Approaching a state shift in Earth's biosphere. *Nature*, 486: 52–58. DOI: 10.1038/nature11018

Bateson, G., 1972. *Steps to an ecology of mind: collected essays in anthropology, psychiatry, evolution, and epistemology*. Chicago: Chicago University Press.

Bauwens, M., 2007. *P2P and human evolution: Peer to peer as the premise of a new mode of civilization*. [online] Available at: <http://www.cybercultura.it/pdf/2005_P2P_bauwens_essay.pdf> [Accessed 1.8.16]

Beck, U., 1992. *Risk society: towards a new modernity*. London: Sage.

Bell, G., 2015. *The answer lies in the soil*, presentation to 12th International Permaculture Conference. London, 9 September.

Bell, M., 2011. Towards pagan agroecology. *Journal of Rural Studies* vol. 27 no. 4: 348–9.

Bellamy Foster, J., 2009. *The Ecological Revolution: Making Peace With The Planet*. New York: Monthly Review Press.

Bellamy Foster, J. and Magdoff, F., 2000. Liebig, Marx, and the Depletion of Soil Fertility: Relevance for Today's Agriculture. In: F. Magdoff, J.B. Foster and F.H. Buttel, eds. *Hungry for profit: the agribusiness threat to farmers, food and the environment*. New York: Monthly Review Press. pp. 43–60.

Bellinger, G. et al., n.d. *Data, information, knowledge, and wisdom* [online] Available at: <http://www.systems-thinking.org/dikw/dikw.htm> [Accessed 3.5.15]

Berkes, F. and Folke, C., 2002. Back to the future: Ecosystem dynamics and local knowledge. In: L.H. Gunderson and C.S. Holling, eds. *Panarchy: Understanding Transformation in Human and Natural Systems*. Washington DC: Island Press.

Bernstein, H., 2013. Food Sovereignty: A skeptical view, conference paper, *Food Sovereignty: A Critical Dialogue*, Yale University, 14–15 September [online] Available at: <https://www.tni.org/files/download/1_bernstein_2013.pdf> [Accessed 1.8.16]

Bettencourt, L. et al., 2007. Growth, innovation, scaling, and the pace of life in cities. *Proceedings of the National Academy of Science U S A*. April 24; vol. 104(no. 17: 7301–06.

Biel, R., 2000. *The new imperialism*. London: Zed Books.

Biel, R., 2012. *The entropy of capitalism*. Leiden: E.J. Brill.

Biel, R., 2013. The future of food. In: S. Bell and J. Paskins, eds. *Imagining the future city: London 2062*. London: Ubiquity Press. pp. 97–106.

Biel, R., 2015a. *Eurocentrism and the communist movement*. Montréal: Kersplebedeb.

Biel, R., 2015b. *The international politics of the 21st century*, originally published as an additional section in Biel, R., 2007. *El nuevo imperialismo – crisis y contradicciones en las relaciones Norte-Sur*. México: Siglo XXI Editores.

Biko, S., 1978. *I write what I like*. London: Heinemann.

Bilalis, D. et al., 2010. Weed-suppressive effects of maize–legume intercropping in organic farming. *International Journal of Pest Management*, vol. 56, no. 2: 173–81.

Bluejay, M., 2013. *Bicycling wastes gas?* blog post, October. [online] Available at: <http://bicycleuniverse.info/transpo/energy.html> [Accessed 10.1.15]

Bolisetty, M.T., Rajadinakaran, G. and Graveley, B.R., 2015. Determining exon connectivity in complex mRNAs by nanopore sequencing. *Genome Biology*, vol. 16 no. 1, DOI: 10.1186/s13059-015-0777-z

Bond, M., 2009. Critical Mass. *New Scientist*, 1 July: 38.

Bourguignon, C. and Bourguignon, L., 2008. *Le sol, la terre et les champs: pour retrouver une agriculture saine*. Paris: Sang de la Terre.

Bowler, P.J., 1976. Malthus, Darwin, and the concept of struggle. *Journal of the History of Ideas*, vol. 37 no. 4, Oct–Dec: 631–50.

Brafman, O. and Beckstrom, R.A., 2006. *The Starfish and the Spider – the Unstoppable Power of Leaderless Organizations*. New York: Penguin.

Brussaard, L. et al., 1997. Biodiversity and ecosystem functioning in soil. *Ambio* (Swedish Academy of Sciences), vol. 26 no. 8 (Dec.) [online] Available at: <http://horizon.documentation.ird.fr/exl-doc/pleins_textes/pleins_textes_6/b_fdi_47-48/010012848.pdf> [Accessed 4.4.15]

Buckminster Fuller, R., 1982. *Critical path*. London: St. Martin's Press.

Burkett, P. and Bellamy Foster, J., 2006. Metabolism, energy and entropy in Marx's critique of political economy: beyond the Podolinski myth. *Theory and Society*, vol. 35.

Business Standard, 2015. Farmer suicides went up to 12,360 in 2014: Report, July 18. [online] Available at: <http://www.business-standard.com/article/economy-policy/farmer-suicides-went-up-to-12-360-in-2014-report-115071800758_1.html> [Accessed 1.8.16]

Buys, J., 1993. Conversion towards organic agriculture in Russia: a preliminary study. *Biological Agriculture and Horticulture*, vol. 10 no. 2: 125–40.

Cabannes, Y. and Delgado, C., 2015. *Another city is possible: alternatives to the city as a commodity – participatory budgeting*. No place of issue: Fondation Charles Leopold Mayer.

Cabell, J.F., and Oelofse, M., 2012. An indicator framework for assessing agroecosystem resilience. *Ecology and Society*, vol. 17 no. 1.

Caldwell, M., 1977. *The wealth of some nations*. London: Zed Books.

Caldwell, M., n.d. *The energy of imperialism, and the imperialism of energy*. London: School of Oriental and African Studies (duplicated).

Calnek, E.E., 1972. Settlement pattern and Chinampa agriculture at Tenochtitlan. *American Antiquity*, vol. 37 no. 1, 104–15.

Capra, F., 1992. *The Tao of physics*. 3rd edition. London: Flamingo.

Carlsson, C., 2008. *Nowtopia: how pirate programmers, outlaw bicyclists and vacant-lot gardeners are inventing the future today!* Edinburgh: AK Press.

Carmona, A. S., 2016. Modern peanut's wild cousin, thought extinct, found in Andes. *Scientific American*, March 22.

Carpenter, S. R. et al., 2015. Allowing variance may enlarge the safe operating space for exploited ecosystems. *Proceedings of the National Academy of Sciences*. DOI: 10.1073/pnas.1511804112

Case, P., 2015. Putin wants Russia to become world leader in organic food. *Farmers' Weekly*, 4 December [online] Available at: <http://www.fwi.co.uk/news/putin-wants-russia-to-become-world-leader-in-organic-food.htm> [Accessed 14.1.16]

Castanas, N., 2014. *Water imperialism: politicising virtual water through entropy theory*. UCL Development Planning Unit, Working Paper no. 161.

Cernansky, R., 2015. The rise of Africa's super vegetables: Long overlooked in parts of Africa, indigenous greens are now capturing attention for their nutritional and environmental benefits. *Nature* 522, 7555, 9 June. [online] Available at: <http://www.nature.com/news/the-rise-of-africa-s-super-vegetables-1.17712> [Accessed 1.8.16]

CGIAR, 2013. *CGIAR Consortium partners with Global Crop Diversity Trust to revitalize genebanks*, 31 Jan. [online] Available at: <http://www.cgiar.org/consortium-news/cgiar-consortium-partners-with-global-crop-diversity-trust-to-revitalize-genebanks/> [Accessed 12.6.14]

Chayanov, A.V., 1966. *On the theory of peasant economy*. Manchester: Manchester University Press.

Chu, C.-C., et al., 2015. Patterns of differential gene expression in adult rotation-resistant and wild-type western corn rootworm digestive tracts. *Evolutionary Applications* DOI: 10.1111/eva.12278

Clark, B. and York, R., 2008. Rifts and shifts: getting to the root of environmental crises. *Monthly Review*, vol. 60, 6 November.

Clark, M., 2013. *Issues of gay/queer identity and sexuality in relation to the development of the theory and practice of environmental movements*, University College London, Dissertation.

Clement, C.R. et al., 2015. The domestication of Amazonia before European conquest. *Proceedings of the Royal Society B* 282: 20150813. [online] Available at: <http://dx.doi.org/10.1098/rspb.2015.0813> [Accessed 1.8.16]

Cleveland, D.A. et al., 2014. Local food hubs for alternative food systems: A case study from Santa Barbara County, California. *Journal of Rural Studies*, vol. 35, July: 26–36.

Climate Heroes, 2014. *Schaduf, watering Cairo's rooftops to life – Sherif Hosny, Tarek Hosny and Abdulraheem Ali bring urban gardens and rooftop agriculture to Cairo in an effort to make all the city greener.* [online] Available at: <http://climateheroes.org/portfolio-item/schaduf-watering-cairos-rooftops-to-life/> [Accessed 1.8.16]

Coeurdray, M. et al., 2015. Rivers and dams of the American empire. Sociology of the environment and the sphere of power. BlueGrass working paper. [online] Available at: <https://www.academia.edu/17473443/RIVERS_AND_DAMS_OF_THE_AMERICAN_EMPIRE._SOCIOLOGY_OF_THE_ENVIRONMENT_AND_THE_SPHERE_OF_POWER>[Accessed 2.12.15]

Coghlan, A., 2006. Whales boast the brain cells that 'make us human'. *New Scientist*, 27 November.

Colectivo La Patria de Chiapas, 2013. *Festival del Jitomate libre*. Poster, June 23.

Committee on Extreme Weather Events and Climate Change Attribution, 2016. *Attribution of extreme weather events in the context of climate change*. Washington DC: National Academies Press.

Conford, P., 1998. A forum for organic husbandry: the new English weekly and agricultural policy, 1939–1949. *Agricultural History Review*, vol. 46:197–201.

Corbalan, J., 2005. Compost de Broussailles. Abécédaire du jardinier bio, *La Gazette des Jardins*, hors-série, October–December.

Cox, S., 2016. *Why growing vegetables in high-rises is wrong on so many levels – The dream of vertical farming is gaining momentum despite many unanswered questions about its feasibility.* AlterNet, 16 February. [online] Available at: <http://www.alternet.org/food/why-growing-vegetables-high-rises-wrong-so-many-levels> [Accessed 20.2.16]

Crouch, D. and Ward, C., 1997. *The allotment – its landscape and culture*. Nottingham: Five Leaves.

Crowther, T.W. et al., 2015. Biotic interactions mediate soil microbial feedbacks to climate change. *Proceedings of the National Academy of Sciences*, 201502956 DOI: 10.1073/pnas.1502956112

Curry, A. and Hodgson, A., 2008. Seeing in multiple horizons: connecting futures to strategy. *Journal of Futures Studies*, vol. 13 no. 1 (August): 1–20.

Dailliez, L., 1981. *Les Templiers et l'agriculture, ou les composts templiers*. Nice: Presses d'Alpes-Méditerranée.

Darwin, C., 1881. *The formation of vegetable mould, through the action of worms*. London: John Murray. [online] Available at: <http://darwin-online.org.uk/converted/pdf/1881_Worms_F1357.pdf> [Accessed 1.8.16]

Davidson-Hunt, I.J. and Berkes, F., 2003. Nature and society through the lens of resilience: toward a human-in-ecosystem perspective. In: F. Berkes, J. Colding and C. Folke, eds. *Navigating social-ecological systems: building resilience for complexity and change.* Cambridge: Cambridge University Press. pp. 53–77.

Davin, E. et al., 2014. No-till farming and climate change. *Proceedings of the National Academy of Sciences*, 8 July, vol. 111 no. 27.

Davis, J.E., 2010. *The Community Land Trust reader*. Lincoln: Institute of Land Policy.

Davis, M.D.,1983. *Game theory – a nontechnical introduction*. Revised edition. New York: Basic Books.

Dawkins, R., 1988. *The blind watchmaker*. London: Penguin.

Decina, S.M. et al., 2016. Soil respiration contributes substantially to urban carbon fluxes in the greater Boston area. *Environmental Pollution*, 212: 433 DOI: 10.1016/j.envpol.2016.01.012

Delaux, P-M. et al., 2015. Algal ancestor of land plants was preadapted for symbiosis. *Proceedings of the National Academy of Sciences*, 201515426 DOI: 10.1073/pnas.1515426112

Deleuze, G. and Guattari, F., 1987. *A thousand plateaus: capitalism and schizophrenia*. Minneapolis: University of Minnesota Press.

de Rosnay, J., 1979. *The macroscope*. New York: Harper & Row.

de Schutter, O., 2010. *Report submitted by the Special Rapporteur on the right to food, Olivier De Schutter, United Nations Human Rights Council, Sixteenth session*. New York: United Nations. 20 December A/HRC/16/49. [online] Available at: <http://www.srfood.org/images/stories/pdf/officialreports/20110308_a-hrc-16-49_agroecology_en.pdf> [Accessed 3.5.14]

de Vries, F.T. et al., 2013. Soil food web properties explain ecosystem services across European land use systems. *Proceedings of the National Academy of Sciences*, vol. 110 no. 35 DOI: 10.1073/pnas.1305198110

Despommier, D., 2013. Farming up the city: the rise of urban vertical farms. *Trends in Biotechnology*, vol. 31 no. 7: 388–389.

Díaz, S. et al., 2015. The global spectrum of plant form and function. *Nature*, 529 (7585): 167 DOI: 10.1038/nature16489

Dincer, I., 2002. The role of exergy in energy policy making. *Energy Policy*, vol. 30 no. 2: 137–49.

Döring, T.F. et al., 2011. Evolutionary plant breeding in cereals – into a new era. *Sustainability*, vol. 3: 1944–71; DOI:10.3390/su3101944n

Doughty, C.E. et al., 2015. Global nutrient transport in a world of giants. *Proceedings of the National Academy of Sciences*, 26 October DOI: 10.1073/pnas.1502549112

Dover, J.W., 2015. *Green infrastructure – incorporating plants and enhancing biodiversity in buildings and urban environments*. London: Routledge.

Dowding, C., 2007. *Organic gardening: the natural no-dig way*. Totnes: Green Books.

Drack, M., 2008. *Ludwig von Bertalanffy's Early System Approach*, von Bertalanffy Lecture, ISSS Conference, Madison WI. [online] Available at: <http://journals.isss.org/index.php/proceedings52nd/article/viewFile/1032/322> [Accessed 11.6.15]

D'Souza, R., n.d. *Global commons: but where is the community?* [online] Available at: <http://www.coloursofresistance.org/414/global-commons-but-where-is-the-community/> [Accessed 3.3.16]

Dummett, E., 2007. *Green Space and Cosmic Order: Le Corbusier's understanding of nature*. University of Edinburgh, PhD thesis. [online] Available at: <https://www.era.lib.ed.ac.uk/bitstream/handle/1842/3236/Emma%20Dummett%20PhD%20thesis%2008.pdf?sequence=2> [Accessed 1.8.16]

Dunbar, R.I.M., 1998. The social brain hypothesis. *Evolutionary Anthropology*, vol. 6: 178–90.

Engel, G.S. et al., 2007. Evidence for wavelike energy transfer through quantum coherence in photosynthetic systems. *Nature*, vol. 446, 12 April: 782–786. DOI:10.1038/nature05678

Engels, F., 1954 [1873–83]. *Dialectics of nature*. 2nd revised edition. Moscow: Progress Publishers.

Engels, F., 1969 [1894]. *Anti-Dühring – Herr Eugen Dühring's revolution in science*. Moscow: Progress Publishers.

Engels, F., 1970 [1877]. *The origin of the family, private property and the state*. Marx and Engels Selected Works Volume 3, Moscow: Progress Publishers.

Engels, F., 1970 [1880] *Socialism: utopian and scientific*. Marx and Engels Selected Works Volume 3, Moscow: Progress Publishers.

Entomological Society of America, 2016. Natural insect control without pesticides. *ScienceDaily*, 20 April. [online] Available at: <www.sciencedaily.com/releases/2016/04/160420111235.htm> [Accessed 1.8.16]

Ettinger, J., 2012. *Seattle Building Massive Edible Forest Filled with Free Food*, 28 February. [online] Available at: <http://www.organicauthority.com/blog/organic/seattle-building-massive-edible-forest-filled-with-free-food/> [Accessed 13 May 2014]

EZLN, n.d. *Autonomous Government I: First-grade textbook for the course 'Freedom according to the Zapatistas', Caracol I: Mother of the Caracoles, Sea of Our Dreams*. [online] Available at: <https://docs.google.com/file/d/0B3RELkjXfmoWb0FzbTd3cHluSXM/edit> [Accessed May 2015]

Fairlie, S., 2010. *Meat – a benign extravagance*. White River Junction VT: Chelsea Green.

Fanon, F., 1952. *Peau noire masques blancs*. Paris: Seuil.

FAO, 2006. *Livestock's long shadow*. Rome: Food and Agriculture Organisation of the United Nations. [online] Available at: <http://www.fao.org/docrep/010/a0701e/a0701e00.HTM> [Accessed 4.11.14]

FAO, 2011. *Save and grow, a new paradigm of agriculture – a policymaker's guide to the sustainable intensification of smallholder crop production*. Rome: Food and Agriculture Organisation of the United Nations. [online] Available at: <http://www.fao.org/docrep/014/i2215e/i2215e.pdf> [Accessed 1.8.16]

FAO, 2012. *The state of food insecurity in the world*. Rome: Food and Agriculture Organisation of the United Nations. [online] Available at: <http://www.fao.org/docrep/016/i3027e/i3027e00.htm> [Accessed 1.8.16]

Federici, S. and George, C., 2013. Commons against and beyond capitalism. *Upping the Anti: a journal of theory and action*. No. 15 (September): 83–97.

Fleming, N., 2014. *Plants talk to each other using an internet of fungus*. [online] Available at: <http://www.bbc.com/earth/story/20141111-plants-have-a-hidden-internet?ocid=twert> [Accessed 4.6.15]

Flint, R.W., 2013. *Practice of sustainable community development: a participatory framework for change*. New York: Springer.

Foley, J.A. et al., 2011. Solutions for a cultivated planet. *Nature*, vol. 478, 20 October.

Forbes, J.D., 1993. *Africans and native Americans – the language of race and the evolution of Red-Black Peoples*. Urbana: University of Illinois Press.

Foucault, M., 2003, *Society must be defended – lectures at the Collège de France 1975–76*. London: Allen Lane.

Fowler, A., 2014. Gardens: why we need to protect Kazakhstan's wild apples. *Guardian*, 8 November.

Frank, A.G., 1978. *World accumulation 1492–1789*. Basingstoke: Macmillan.

Frankfurter Allgemeiner Zeitung, 2011. *Im Gespräch: Alexander Kluge: Karl Marx ist der Dichter unserer Krise*, 27 July. [online] Available at: <http://www.faz.net/aktuell/feuilleton/im-gespraech-alexander-kluge-karl-marx-ist-der-dichter-unserer-krise-1714137.html> [Accessed 4.8.16]

Freire, P., 1972. *Pedagogy of the oppressed*. Harmondsworth: Penguin.

Fukuoka, M., 1978. *The one-straw revolution: an introduction to natural farming*. Emmaus PA: Rodale.

Galeano, S., 2015, *The storm, the sentinel, and night watch syndrome*. Mexico, April. [online] Available at: <http://enlacezapatista.ezln.org.mx/2015/04/04/the-storm-the-sentinel-and-night-watch-syndrome/> [Accessed 21.1.16]

Gatti, R.C., 2016. A conceptual model of new hypothesis on the evolution of biodiversity. *Biologia*, vol. 71 no. 3: 343–51, DOI: 10.1515/biolog-2016-0032

Gedge, D., 2013, presentation at workshop on *Green Roof Avant-Garde*, Garden Museum, London, 3 June.

Geels, F.W. and Schot, J., 2007. Typology of sociotechnical transition pathways. *Research Policy*, vol. 36: 399–417.

Geoghan, V., 2008. *Utopianism and Marxism*. Bern: Peter Lang.

Gersper, P.S. et al., 1993. Soil conservation in Cuba: A key to the new model for agriculture. *Agriculture and Human Values*, vol. 10 no. 3, June: 16–23.

Gharajedaghi, J., 2006. *Systems thinking: managing chaos and complexity*. Burlington MA: Butterworth-Heinemann.

Giannattasio, M. et al., 2013. Microbiological features and bioactivity of a fermented manure product (Preparation 500) used in biodynamic agriculture. *Journal of Microbiology and Biotechnology*, vol. 23 no 5: 644–51.

Giesa, T., Spivak, D.I. and Buehler, M.J., 2011. Reoccurring patterns in hierarchical protein materials and music: the power of analogies. *BioNanoScience*, vol. 1: 153–61.

Ginelli, F. et al., 2015. Intermittent collective dynamics emerge from conflicting imperatives in sheep herds. *Proceedings of the National Academy of Sciences* 201503749 DOI: 10.1073/pnas.1503749112

Girardet, H., ed. 1976. *Land for the people*. London: Crescent Books.

Girardet, H. and Mendonça, M., 2009. *A renewable world – energy, ecology, equality*. Totnes: Green Books.

Glaeser, B., (ed.) 1987. *The Green Revolution Revisited – Critique and Alternatives*. London: Allen and Unwin.

Glaeser, B. and Phillips-Howard, K., 1987. Low-energy farming systems in Nigeria. In: B. Glaeser, ed. *The Green Revolution revisited – critique and alternatives*. London: Allen and Unwin.

Global Alliance for the Rights of Nature, 2015. *Peoples' Tribunal Convention for the Establishment of the International Rights of Nature Tribunal* 4 December. [online] Available at: <http://therightsofnature.org/peoples-convention-tribunal/> [Accessed 1.3.16]

Goldenberg, S., 2015. The doomsday vault: the seeds that could save a post-apocalyptic world. *Guardian* 20 May. [online] Available at: <http://www.theguardian.com/science/2015/may/20/the-doomsday-vault-seeds-save-post-apocalyptic-world> [Accessed 1.8.16]

Goodall, C., 2014. *Walking can be more carbon-intensive than driving*, blog post 22 July. [online] Available at: <http://www.carboncommentary.com/blog/2014/07/22/walking-can-be-more-carbon-intensive-than-driving?rq=walking> [Accessed 11.12.15]

Goonatilake, S., 1984. *Aborted discovery – science and creativity in the third world*. London: Zed Books.

Gore, C., 2008. Healthy urban food production and local government. In: D. Cole, et al., eds. *Healthy city harvests – generating evidence to guide policy on urban agriculture*. Lima, Peru: Urban Harvest/Makerere University Press. pp 49–65.

Gould, S.J. and Eldredge, N., 1977. Punctuated equilibria: the tempo and mode of evolution reconsidered. *Paleobiology*, vol. 3 no. 2. (Spring): 115–51.

GRAIN, 2016. *The Great Climate Robbery – how the food system drives climate change and what we can do about it*. No place of issue: Daraja Press.

Gramsci, A., 1971 [1927–33]. *Selections from prison notebooks*. London: Lawrence and Wishart.

Grant, T. and Woods, A., 1995. *Reason in revolt: Marxist philosophy and modern science*. [online] Available at: <http://www.marxist.com/rircontents.htm> [Accessed 7.4.14]

Graziano da Silva, J., 2015, *Agriculture must change – FAO Director-General speaks at International Forum on Agriculture and Climate Change*, Paris 20 February [online] Available at: <http://www.fao.org/news/story/en/item/278192/icode/> [Accessed 15.3.15]

Grossmann, I., et al., 2016. A heart and a mind: self-distancing facilitates the association between heart rate variability, and wise reasoning. *Frontiers in Behavioral Neuroscience*. April.

Growing Communities, n.d. *Our organic fruit and veg bag scheme* [online] Available at: <http://www.growingcommunities.org/organic-veg-scheme/> [Accessed 1.8.16]

Gunderson, L.H. and Holling, C.S., 2002. *Panarchy – understanding transformation in human and natural systems*. Washington DC: Island Press.

Günther, G., 1964. *Cybernetics and the dialectic materialism of Marx and Lenin*, lecture at University of Cologne, 17 July. In: G. Günther (ed. Rudolf Kaehr) *Cyberphilosophy*, web edition (2004). [online] Available at: <http://www.thinkartlab.com/pkl/archive/Cyberphilosophy.pdf> [Accessed 11.4.15]

Hancox, D., 2016. Gentrification X: how an academic argument became the people's protest. *Guardian* 12 January [online] Available at: <http://www.theguardian.com/cities/2016/jan/12/gentrification-argument-protest-backlash-urban-generation-displacement?CMP=fb_a-cities_b-gdncities> [Accessed 11.4.15]

Hardin, G., 1968. The tragedy of the commons. *Science*, 162: 1243–8.

Hartsock, N., 1983. *Money, sex and power – toward a feminist historical materialism*. New York: Longman.

Hayek, F.A., 1964. The theory of complex phenomena. In: M. Bunge, ed. *The critical approach to science and philosophy*. London: Collier-Macmillan.

Hegel, G.W.F., 1969. *The science of logic*, trans. A.V. Miller. London: George Allen and Unwin.

Hegel, G.W.F., 1995. *Lectures on the history of philosophy*, volume 1; trans. E.S. Haldane, Lincoln NE: University of Nebraska Press. pp. 278ff. [online] Available at: <https://www.marxists.org/reference/archive/hegel/works/hp/hpheraclitus.htm> [Accessed 1.8.16]

Henry, R., 2015. interview in *New Scientist*, No. 3044, 24 October.

Heylighen, F., 2008. Complexity and self-organization. In: M.J. Bates and M.N. Maack, *Encyclopedia of library and information sciences*. London: Taylor & Francis.

Heynen, N., 2015. Urban political ecology II: the abolitionist century. *Progress in Human Geography*: 1–7 DOI: 10.1177/0309132515617394.

Higgins, S.I. and Scheiter, S., 2012. Atmospheric CO2 forces abrupt vegetation shifts locally, but not globally. *Nature* DOI:10.1038/nature11238 Published online 27 June.

Hirt, S. and Zahm, D., 2012. *The urban wisdom of Jane Jacobs*. London: Routledge.

Ho, M-W., 1998. *The rainbow and the worm: the physics of organisms*. Singapore: World Scientific.

Hobbs, S., 1976. Theory and practice. In: H. Girardet, ed. *Land for the people*. London: Crescent Books.

Hobson, J.A., 1902. *Imperialism – a study*. New York: James Pott & Co.

Hodgson, J., with Hopkins, R., 2010. *Transition in action, Totnes 2030, an energy descent action plan*. Totnes: Transition Town. [online] Sourced from: <http://totnesedap.org.uk/book/part3/vision-totnes-district-2030/a-forest-model-of-society/> [Accessed 13.12.12. Note: this web page is no longer active]

Holland, G.J. and Webster, P.J., 2007. Heightened tropical cyclone activity in the North Atlantic: natural variability or climate trend? *Philosophical Transactions of the Royal Society A* 365: 2695–716.

Holling, C.S., 2001. Understanding the complexity of economic, ecological, and social systems. *Ecosystems* vol. 4: 390–405.

Holling, C.S., Gunderson, L.H. and Ludwig, D., 2002. In quest of a theory of adaptive change. In: L.H. Gunderson and C.S. Holling eds. *Panarchy – understanding transformation in human and natural systems*. Washington DC: Island Press.

Holmgren, D., 1990. *Aboriginal land use*, presentation to RMIT (University of Technology) Melbourne, March. [online] Available at: <http://www.unigaia-brasil.org/pdfs/david-Holmgren/04AbLand.pdf> [Accessed 5.6.15]

Holmgren, D., 1994. *The ethics and principles of permaculture*. Talk at Tir Penrhos Isaf, transcribed by Chris Dixon. [online] Available at: <http://www.konsk.co.uk/resource/holm2.htm> [Accessed 1.8.16]

Holt-Giménez, E. and Patel, R., 2009. *Food rebellions! Crisis and hunger for justice*. Cape Town: Pambazuka Press.

Hopkins, R., 2015. Keynote speech, IPCUK, London, 9 September.

Hornborg, A., 2001. *The power of the machine – global inequalities of economy, technology, and environment*. Lanham MD: Rowman & Littlefield.

Hospes, O., 2014. Food sovereignty: the debate, the deadlock, and a suggested detour. *Agriculture and Human Values* 31: 119–30.

Hough, A., 2010. Britain facing food crisis as world's soil 'vanishes in 60 years'. *Daily Telegraph* 3 February.

Howard, A., 1943. *An agricultural testament*. New York: Oxford University Press.

Howard, E., 2012 [1902]. *Garden cities of tomorrow*. Barsinghausen: Unikum Verlag.

Hug, L.A. et al., 2016. A new view of the tree of life. *Nature Microbiology* 16048 DOI: 10.1038/nmicrobiol.2016.48

Hundertwasser, F., 1964 [1958]. *Mouldiness manifesto against rationalism in architecture*, revised version. [online] Available at: <http://www.hundertwasser.com/english/texts/philo_verschimmelungsmanifest.php> [Accessed 1.8.16]

Ilyenkov, E.V., 1982 [1961]. *The dialectics of the abstract and the concrete in Marx's Capital*. Moscow: Foreign Languages Press.

IME, 2013. *Global food – waste not want not*, London: Institution of Mechnical Engineers. [online] Available at: <http://www.imeche.org/docs/default-source/reports/Global_Food_Report.pdf?sfvrsn=0> [Accessed 6.8.14]

Indoor Harvest Corp., 2015. *Indoor Harvest Corp. Set to Design-Build World's First Publicly-Owned, Open Data, Crowdfunded, Vertical Farm Research and Education Campus*, Dec. 2. [online] Available at: <https://globenewswire.com/news-release/2015/12/02/792403/0/en/Indoor-Harvest-Corp-Set-to-Design-Build-World-s-First-Publicly-Owned-Open-Data-Crowdfunded-Vertical-Farm-Research-and-Education-Campus.html> [Accessed 4.8.16]

Institute of Photonic Sciences, 2013. Uncovering quantum secret in photosynthesis. *ScienceDaily*, 20 June. [online] Available at: <http://www.sciencedaily.com/releases/2013/06/130620142932.htm> [Accessed 11.1.15]

Instituto Permacultura Ná Lu'um, 2013. Poster, 5 May. Source: Línea de Fuego, personal communication.

International Biochar Initiative, n.d. *What is Open Source Technology, and how important is it to the emerging biochar industry?* [online] Available at: <http://www.biochar-international.org/technology/opensource>[Accessed 30.1.16]

Ioffe, G., 2005. The downsizing of Russian agriculture. *Europe-Asia Studies*, vol. 57, no. 2, March: 179–208.

IPCC, 2014. *Climate change 2014: impacts, adaptation, and vulnerability*. [online] Available at: <http://ipcc-wg2.gov/AR5/images/uploads/IPCC_WG2AR5_SPM_Approved.pdf> [Accessed 4.11.15]

Isbell, F. et al., 2015. Biodiversity increases the resistance of ecosystem productivity to climate extremes. *Nature*, DOI: 10.1038/nature15374

Jackson, C., 1993. Women/nature or gender/history? A critique of ecofeminist 'development'. *Journal of Peasant Studies*, vol. 20 no. 3, 389–418.

Jackson, W., 2002. Natural systems agriculture: a radical alternative. *Agriculture, Ecosystems and Environment*, vol. 88: 111–17.

Jacobsohn, A., 2016. Introduction. In: J.-G. Moreau and J.-J. Daverne, 2016 [1843]. *Manuel pratique de la culture maraîchère de Paris*. Paris: Editions du Linteau.

Jing, X., et al., 2015. The links between ecosystem multifunctionality and above- and belowground biodiversity are mediated by climate. *Nature Communications*, vol. 6: 8159 DOI: 10.1038/NCOMMS9159

Jones, M., 2001. *Stand-off between Opec and Russia?* (posting to email discussion forum) 20 November. [online] Available at: <http://wsarch.ucr.edu/wsnmail/2001/msg01791.html> [Accessed 4.11.10]

Joseph, J. et al., 2002. Short duration grazing research in Africa – an extensive review of the Charter Grazing Trials and other short duration grazing studies on African rangelands. *Rangelands*, vol. 24 no. 2 [online] Available from: <https://journals.uair.arizona.edu/index.php/rangelands/article/view/11560/10833> [Accessed 1.8.16]

Jung, S.C. et al., 2012. Mycorrhiza-induced resistance and priming of plant defenses. *Journal of Chemical Ecology*, vol. 38 no. 6 (June): pp. 651–64.

Kadas, G., 2006. Rare invertebrates colonizing green roofs in London. *Urban Habitats*, December.

Kang, N.-Y. and Elsner, J.B., 2015. Trade-off between intensity and frequency of global tropical cyclones. *Nature Climate Change*, DOI: 10.1038/nclimate2646

KQED News, 2015. California is sinking. [online] Video: Available at: <https://www.facebook.com/KQEDnews/videos/903293236411741/> [Accessed 10.3.16]

King, D., 1996. An Interview with Professor Brian Goodwin. *GenEthics News*, Issue 11, March/April: 6–8. [online] Available at: <http://ngin.tripod.com/article8.htm> [Accessed 3.8.12]

Klinger, C.R. et al., 2016. Ecological genomics of mutualism decline in nitrogen-fixing bacteria. *Proceedings of the Royal Society B*, vol. 283 no. 1826, 20152563 DOI: 10.1098/rspb.2015.2563

Kluge, A., 2008. *Nachrichten aus der ideologischen Antike – Marx/Eisenstein/Das Kapital*, feature film.

Krasil'nikov, N.A., 1961 [1958]. *Soil microorganisms and higher plants*, Moscow Academy of Sciences of the USSR, trans. for National Science Foundation, Washington DC and Department of Agriculture.

Kropotkin, P., 1892. *The conquest of bread*. [online] Available at: <http://dwardmac.pitzer.edu/Anarchist_Archives/kropotkin/conquest/ch5.html> [Accessed 10.11.15]

Kuhn, T., 1970. *The structure of scientific revolutions*. 2nd enlarged edition. Chicago: University of Chicago Press.

Kyndt, T. et al., 2015. The genome of cultivated sweet potato contains Agrobacterium T-DNAs with expressed genes: an example of a naturally transgenic food crop. *Proceedings of the National Academy of Sciences*, vol. 112 no. 18, 5844–9, DOI: 10.1073/pnas.1419685112

L.A. Green Grounds, n.d. [online] Available at: <http://lagreengrounds.org/about/> [Accessed 13 May 2014].

Lagi, M., Bertrand, K.Z. and Bar-Yam, Y., 2011. The food crises and political instability in North Africa and the Middle East. *arXiv*: 1108.2455, 10 August.

Lal, R., 2004. Soil carbon sequestration impacts on global climate change and food security. *Science*, 304.

Landon, A.J., 2008. The 'how' of the three sisters: the origins of agriculture in Mesoamerica and the human niche. *Nebraska Anthropologist*. Paper 40. [online] Downloadable from: <http://digitalcommons.unl.edu/nebanthro/40> [Accessed 1.8.16]

Le Page, M., 2016a. Farming has made GMOs for millennia. *New Scientist* 12 March.

Le Page, M., 2016b. Meet your maker. *New Scientist*, 12 August. Collected in *Origin, evolution, extinction – the epic story of life on Earth. New Scientist: The collection*, book 3. London: Reed.

Lehmann, J., Coumou, D. and Frieler, K., 2015. Increased record-breaking precipitation events under global warming. *Climatic Change*, DOI: 10.1007/s10584-015-1434-y

Leigh, G.J., 2004. *The world's greatest fix – a history of nitrogen in agriculture*. Oxford: Oxford University Press.

Lenin, V.I., 1937 [1920]. Once again on the trade unions, the present situation and the mistakes of Trotsky and Bukharin. *Lenin selected works*, volume 9. Moscow: Co-operative Publishing Society of Foreign Workers.

Lenin, V.I., 1939. *Imperialism, the highest stage of capitalism*, New York: International Publishers.

Lenin, V.I., 1972 [1908]. *Materialism and empirio-criticism*. Peking: Foreign Languages Press.

Lenin, V.I., 1972 [1914–16]. Conspectus of Hegel's book The Science of Logic. Lenin *Collected Works*, volume 38 (Philosophical Notebooks), Moscow: Progress Publishers.

Levins, R., 2004. *How Cuba is going ecological*. Latin American Studies Association meetings, October 6–10.

Levins, R. and Lewontin, R., 1980. Dialectics and reductionism in ecology. *Synthese*, vol. 43: 47–78.

Liebmann, M.J. et al., 2016. Native American depopulation, reforestation, and fire regimes in the Southwest United States, 1492–1900 CE. *Proceedings of the National Academy of Sciences*, 201521744 DOI: 10.1073/pnas.1521744113

Li, D. and Waller, D., 2015. Drivers of observed biotic homogenization in pine barrens of central Wisconsin. *Ecology*, vol. 96 no. 4: 1030 DOI: 10.1890/14-0893.1

Lifespan, 2016. Community food bank study dispels belief healthy diets are costly: research shows that such diets are less costly when compared to the cheapest USDA-recommended diet. *ScienceDaily*. 5 January. [online] Available at: <www.sciencedaily.com/releases/2016/01/160105101744.htm> [Accessed 1.8.16]

Lin, C. et al., 2015. Impacts of wind stilling on solar radiation variability in China. *Nature Scientific Reports*, vol. 5 no: 15135 DOI:10.1038/srep15135

Lin, Y. et al., 2015. Combinatorial gene regulation by modulation of relative pulse timing. *Nature*, vol. 527 no. 7576; DOI: 10.1038/nature15710

Linear, M., 1985. *Zapping the third world – the disaster of development aid*. London: Pluto.

Litherland, R., 2010. *Where next for the community food movement?* duplicated. [online] Available at: <https://www.organiclea.org.uk/about/publications/> [Accessed 5.8.16]

Liu, C. et al., 2015. Nanowire–bacteria hybrids for unassisted solar carbon dioxide fixation to value-added chemicals. *Nano Letters*, vol. 15 no. 5, 150407103432009 DOI: 10.1021/acs.nanolett.5b01254

Liu, J. et al., 2015. Metabolic co-dependence gives rise to collective oscillations within biofilms. *Nature*, vol. 523 DOI: 10.1038/nature14660

Lobell, D.B. and Field, C.B., 2007. Global scale climate–crop yield relationships and the impacts of recent warming. *Environmental Research Letters*, vol. 2 no. 1.

London Orchard Project, n.d. [online] Available at: <http://thelondonorchardproject.org/> [Accessed 20.6.13].

Lott, M.C., 2011. 10 calories in, 1 calorie out: the energy we spend on food. *Scientific American* blog post, 11 August. [online] Available at: <http://blogs.scientific-american.com/plugged-in/2011/08/11/10-calories-in-1-calorie-out-the-energy-we-spend-on-food/> [Accessed 13 May 2014].

Lovelock, J., 2000. *The ages of Gaia*. 2nd edition, revised with new preface and corrections. Oxford: Oxford University Press.

Lu, X., Wang, L. and McCabe, M.F., 2016. Elevated CO2 as a driver of global dryland greening. *Scientific Reports*, vol. 6: 20716 DOI: 10.1038/srep20716

Lucas, C., 2005. *Perturbation and transients – the edge of chaos*. Published online by Complexity and Artificial Life Research Concept for Self-Organizing Systems (CALRESCO). http://www.calresco.org/perturb.htm [Accessed 6.7.11 but website is now no longer active].

Luxemburg, R., 1913. *Die Akkumulation des Kapitals – eine Beitrag zur Ökonomischen Erklärung des Imperialismus*. Berlin: Paul Singer.

Lyson, T.A., 2004. *Civic agriculture: reconnecting farm, food, and community*. Lebanon NH: Tufts University Press.

McGuirk, J., 2015. Urban commons have radical potential – it's not just about community gardens. *Guardian* 15 June.

McHenry, M.P., 2009. Agricultural bio-char production, renewable energy generation and farm carbon sequestration in Western Australia: certainty, uncertainty and risk. *Agriculture, Ecosystems & Environment*, vol. 129 no. 1–3. [online] Available at: <http://researchrepository.murdoch.edu.au/3675/1/Agricultural_bio-char_production.pdf> [Accessed 1.8.16]

McKay, G., 2011. *Radical gardening*. London: Frances Lincoln.

McMichael, C. H. et al., 2014. Predicting pre-Columbian anthropogenic soils in Amazonia, *Proceedings of the Royal Society B*, 8 January DOI: 10.1098/rspb.2013.2475

McNeill, J. R. and Winiwarter, V., 2004. Breaking the sod: humankind, history, and soil. *Science*, vol. 304: 1629.

Mao, Z., 1977 [1956]. On the ten major relationships. *Mao Tse-tung Selected Works*, vol. 5. Beijing: Foreign Languages Press.

Mares, T.M. and Peña, D.G., 2010. Urban agriculture in the making of insurgent spaces in Los Angeles and Seattle. In: J. Hou, ed. *Insurgent public space – guerrilla urbanism and the remaking of contemporary cities*. London: Routledge.

Marsden, T. and Morley, A., 2014. Current food questions and their scholarly challenges – creating and framing a sustainable food paradigm. In: T. Marsden and A. Morley, eds. *Sustainable food systems: building a new paradigm*. Abingdon: Routledge.

Martin, A.R. and Isaac, M.E., 2015. Plant functional traits in agroecosystems: a blueprint for research. *Journal of Applied Ecology*, vol. 52 no. 6 DOI: 10.1111/1365-2664.12526

Martinez-Alier, J., 2011. The EROI of agriculture and its use by the Via Campesina. *Journal of Peasant Studies*, vol. 38: 145–60.

Marx, K., 1954 [1887]. *Capital* vol. 1. Moscow: Progress Publishers.

Marx, K., 1969 [1852]. *The eighteenth Brumaire of Louis Bonaparte.* Marx and Engels Selected Works, vol. I. Moscow: Progress Publishers.

Marx, K., 1969 [1865]. *Wages, Price and Profit.* Marx and Engels Selected Works, vol. 2, Moscow: Progress Publishers.

Marx, K., 1973 [1857–8]. *Grundrisse – foundations of the critique of political economy.* London: Penguin Books.

Marx, K. and Engels, F., 1968. *Karl Marx-Friedrich Engels-Werke*, Band 23, "Das Kapital", Bd. I, Dritter Abschnitt. Berlin: Dietz Verlag, reproduced [online] Available at: <http://www.mlwerke.de/me/me23/me23_192.htm#Kap_5_1> [Accessed 5.1.15]

Marx, K. and Engels, F., 1969 [1848]. *Manifesto of the Communist Party.* Marx and Engels Selected Works, vol. I. Moscow: Progress Publishers.

Mason, P., 2015. The end of capitalism has begun. *The Guardian*, 17 July. [online] Available at: <http://www.theguardian.com/books/2015/jul/17/postcapitalism-end-of-capitalism-begun> [Accessed 1.8.16]

Massachusetts Institute of Technology, 2016. Bacteria, electrons spin in similar patterns: bacteria streaming through a lattice behave like electrons in a magnetic material. *ScienceDaily*, 5 January. [online] Available at: <www.sciencedaily.com/releases/2016/01/160105133132.htm> [Accessed 7.1.16]

Merchant, C., 1980. *The death of nature – women, ecology and the scientific revolution.* San Francisco: Harper.

Michelson, M., 2015. *Botanical gardens to feed the world.* California Academy of Sciences 1 June.

Mies, M. and Shiva, V., eds. 1993. *Ecofeminism.* Halifax, Nova Scotia: Fernwood Publications.

Millennium Ecosystem Assessment, 2005. *Ecosystems and human well-being: synthesis.* Washington DC: Island Press.

Mirolo, A., 2011. *Philippe Pétain, Maréchal de France, ses années noires de 1940 à 1944*, blog post, 4 February [online] Available at: <http://blogs.mediapart.fr/blog/anido-mirolo/040211/philippe-petain-marechal-de-france-ses-annees-noires-de-1940-1944-suit> [Accessed 20 May 2014].

Monbiot, G., 2010. I was wrong about veganism. Let them eat meat – but farm it properly. *The Guardian*, 6 September [online] Available at: <http://www.theguardian.com/commentisfree/2010/sep/06/meat-production-veganism-deforestation> [Accessed 1.8.16]

Montgomery, D.R., 2007. *Dirt – the erosion of civilisations.* Berkeley: University of California Press.

Montgomery, D.R., 2008. Peak soil. *New Internationalist*, issue 418.

Moore, J.H. et al., 2016. Fruit gardens enhance mammal diversity and biomass in a Southeast Asian rainforest. *Biological Conservation*. Volume 194 (February): 132–138.

Mora, C. et al., 2015. Suitable days for plant growth disappear under projected climate change: potential human and biotic vulnerability. *PLoS Biology*, 10 June, DOI: 10.1371/journal.pbio.1002167

Morin, E., 1979. *From the concept of system to the paradigm of complexity*, translation of *Le système, paradigme ou théorie?* Address, Versailles 21 November, trans. Sean Kelly. [online] Available at: <https://manoftheword.files.wordpress.com/2013/07/morin-paradigm-of-complexity.pdf> [Accessed 5.3.15]

Morin, E., 2008. *On complexity.* Creskill NJ: Hampton Press.

Morin, E., Rabhi, P., Rinpoché, D. and Pech, A., 2012. *Une vision spirituelle de la crise économique – altruisme plutôt qu'avidité : le remède à la crise.* Paris: Yves Michel Editions.

Mouhot, J.-F., 2010. We are all slave owners now: fossil fuels, energy consumption and the legacy of slave abolition. In: M. Levene, R. Johnson and P. Roberts, eds. *History at the end of the world.* Penrith: Humanities Ebooks.

Nabham, G.P., 2009. *Where our food comes from: retracing Nikolay Vavilov's quest to end famine.* Washington DC: Island Press.

NASA/Jet Propulsion Laboratory, 2015. Excitement grows as NASA carbon sleuth begins Year Two. *ScienceDaily*, 29 October. [online] Available at: <www.sciencedaily.com/releases/2015/10/151029185457.htm> [Accessed 1.8.16]

Neocleous, M., 2013. Resisting resilience. *Radical Philosophy,* vol. 178 Mar/Apr.
Netherlands Institute of Ecology, 2012. Voicemail discovered in nature: Insects receive soil messages from the past. *ScienceDaily,* 12 June. [online] Available at: <www.sciencedaily.com/releases/2012/06/120612115946.htm> [Accessed 1.8.16]
Noble, D., 2006. *The music of life: biology beyond genes.* Oxford: Oxford University Press.
North Carolina State University. 2015. Study finds key molecular mechanism regulating plant translational activity: Response to ethylene, important hormone, shown. *ScienceDaily.* 22 October. [online] Available at: www.sciencedaily.com/releases/2015/10/151022124524.htm
Nowak, M., 2006. Five rules for the evolution of cooperation. *Science,* vol. 314. 8 December: 1560–3.
Odum, E.P., 1969. The strategy of ecosystem development – an understanding of ecological succession provides a basis for resolving man's conflict with nature. *Science,* vol. 164, no. 3877: 262–70.
O'Hagan, E.M., 2015. Mass migration is no 'crisis': it's the new normal as the climate changes. *The Guardian,* 18 August. [online] Available at: <http://www.theguardian.com/commentisfree/2015/aug/18/mass-migration-crisis-refugees-climate-change> [Accessed 20.8.15]
Olvera-Gonzalez, E. et al., 2013. Intelligent lighting system for plant growth and development. *Computers and Electronics in Agriculture,* vol. 92: 48–53.
OrganicLea, 2014: *March programme of events,* by email.
Ostrom, E., 2005. *Understanding institutional diversity.* Princeton: Princeton University Press.
Palomino, H., 2003. Las experiencias actuales de autogestión en Argentina. *Nueva Sociedad,* vol. 184: 115–28.
Patel, R., 2008. *Stuffed and starved: markets, power and the hidden battle for the world's food system.* New Jersey: Melville House.
Paustian, K. et al., 2016. Climate-smart soils. *Nature,* vol. 532 no. 7597: 49 DOI: 10.1038/nature17174
Peacock, A.J., 1969. *Bradford Chartism.* York: St. Anthony's Press.
Penn State University, 2016. Carbon dioxide stored underground can find multiple ways to escape. *ScienceDaily,* 11 February. [online] Available at: <www.sciencedaily.com/releases/2016/02/160211185935.htm> [Accessed 1.8.16]
Penrose, R., 2010. *Cycles of time.* London: The Bodley Head.
Perelman, M., 1987. *Marx's crises theory – scarcity, labor and finance.* New York: Praeger.
Phillips, S.L. and Wolfe, M.S., 2005. Evolutionary plant breeding for low input systems. *Journal of Agricultural Science,* vol. 143, 245–54.
Pierce, F., 2015. Over a barrel. *New Scientist,* no. 3004, 17 January.
Pierce, F., 2016. Hello, cool world. *New Scientist,* no. 3061, 20 February.
Piff, P.K. et al., 2015. Awe, the small self, and prosocial behavior. *Journal of Personality and Social Psychology,* vol. 108 no. 6: 883 DOI: 10.1037/pspi0000018
Pillot, J.-J. et al., 1979 [1840]. Premier banquet communiste le 1er juillet 1840. In: G.M. Bravo, ed. *Socialistes avant Marx,* Tome II. Paris: Maspero.
Pinderhughes, R., 2004. *Alternative urban futures – planning for sustainable development in cities throughout the world.* Lanham MD: Rowman and Littlefield.
Pinkerton, T. and Hopkins, R., 2009. *Local food: how to make it happen in your community.* Totnes: Transition Books.
Plantagon, n.d. *Owners and founders.* [online] Available at: <http://plantagon.com/about/governance/owners> [Accessed 3.3.16]
Polanyi, K., 1944. *The great transformation.* New York: Rinehart & Company.
Polanyi, M., 1962. *The tacit dimension.* New York: Doubleday.
Pontzer, H. et al., 2012. Hunter-gatherer energetics and human obesity. *PLoS ONE,* vol. 7 no. 7: e40503 DOI: 10.1371/journal.pone.0040503
Potter, C. and Tilzey, M., 2005. Agricultural policy discourses in the European post-Fordist transition: neoliberalism, neomercantilism and multifunctionality. *Progress in Human Geography,* vol. 29 no. 5: 581–600.
Pouvreau, D., 2009. *The dialectical tragedy of the concept of wholeness: Ludwig von Bertalanffy's biography revisited. Volume 1: Exploring unity through diversity.* New York: ISCE Publishing.
Powers, S.M. et al., 2016. Long-term accumulation and transport of anthropogenic phosphorus in three river basins. *Nature Geoscience,* vol. 9 DOI: 10.1038/ngeo2693
Prigogine, I., 2003. *Is future given?* Singapore: World Scientific.

Prigogine, I. and Stengers, I., 1985. *Order out of chaos.* London: Flamingo.

Prindle, A. et al., 2015. Ion channels enable electrical communication in bacterial communities. *Nature,* vol. 527 DOI: 10.1038/nature15709

Purdue University, 2016. Market integration could help protect poor from climate-related food insecurity. *ScienceDaily,* 18 February. [online] Available at: <www.sciencedaily.com/releases/2016/02/160218135036.htm> [Accessed 1.8.16]

Puttnam, H. et al., 2014. Coupling Agroecology and PAR to Identify Appropriate Food Security and Sovereignty Strategies in Indigenous Communities. *Agroecology and Sustainable Food Systems* 38, 2: 165–198.

Quesnay, F., 1888. *Oeuvres economiques et philosophiques.* Frankfurt (Joseph Baer et cie) [online] Available at: <http://gallica.bnf.fr/ark:/12148/bpt6k72832q/f6.image> [Accessed 5.8.16]

Rabagliati, M., 2014. *Solar Panel Making Workshop for Loughborough Residents,* blog post, 18 November. [online] Available at: <https://brixtonenergy.co.uk/solar-panel-making-workshop-for-loughborough-residents/> [Accessed 1.8.16]

Redclift, M., 1987. Raised bed agriculture in pre-Columbian Central and South America – a traditional solution to the problem of "sustainable" farming systems. *Biological Agriculture and Horticulture,* vol. 5 no. 1: 51–9.

Rees, W.E., 2010. Thinking resilience. In: R. Heinberg and D. Lerch, eds. *The post carbon reader: managing the 21st century's sustainability crises.* Healdsburg CA: Watershed Media.

Reynolds, P.J., 1985. Carbonised seed, crop yield, weed infestation and harvesting techniques of the Iron Age. *Les techniques de conservation des grains à long terme 3.1* Paris: CNRS: 397–407.

Reynolds, P.J. and Shaw, C.E., 1999. The third harvest of the first millenium AD in the Plana de Vic. *Actes del Congres Internacional Gilbert d'Orlhac i el seu temps : Catalunya i Europa a la fin del premier millenni.* Vic (Spain), Eumo Editorial, reproduced [online] Available at: <http://www.butser.org.uk/iafhpa_16_hcc.html> [Accessed 2.9.14]

Reynolds, R., 2008. *On guerrilla gardening – a handbook for gardening without boundaries.* London: Bloomsbury.

Ricardo, D., 1951. *On the principles of political economy and taxation – the works and correspondence of David Ricardo* ed. P. Sraffa, vol. I. Cambridge: Cambridge University Press.

Richards, P., 1985. *Indigenous agricultural revolution – ecology and food production in West Africa.* London: Hutchinson.

Roach, J., 2008. Superdirt made lost Amazon cities possible. *National Geographic News,* 19 November.

Rodale Institute, 2014. *Regenerative organic agriculture and climate change.* [online] Available at: <http://rodaleinstitute.org/assets/RegenOrgAgricultureAndClimateChange_20140418.pdf> [Accessed 2.4.13]

Roederer, J.G., 2003. On the concept of information and its role in nature. *Entropy,* vol. 5 no. 1.

Rosset, P., 1996. *Cuba: alternative agriculture during crisis.* Washington DC: World Resources Institute, September.

Rostow, W.W., 1958. The take-off into self-sustained growth. In: A.N. Agarwala and S.P. Singh, eds. *The economics of underdevelopment.* Delhi: Oxford University Press. pp. 154–86.

Sadler, R.C., 2016. Strengthening the core, improving access: bringing healthy food downtown via a farmers' market move. *Applied Geography,* vol. 67: 119 DOI: 10.1016/j.apgeog.2015.12.010

SAGE (Sustainable Agriculture Education), n.d. [online] Available at: <http://www.sage-center.org/projects/new-ruralism-framework-foodshed-assessments-for-metro-regions/> [Accessed 4.10.12].

Salk Institute, 2015. Basic understanding of plants: cellular damage control system helps plants tough it out. *ScienceDaily,* 22 October. [online] Available at: <www.sciencedaily.com/releases/2015/10/151022161120.htm> [Accessed 1.8.16]

Sanjari, G. et al., 2008. Comparing the effects of continuous and time-controlled grazing systems on soil characteristics in Southeast Queensland. *Soil Research,* vol. 46 no. 4: 348–58.

Scharf, C., 2012. *Gravity's engines – the other side of black holes.* London: Allen Lane.

Scheffer, M. and Carpenter, S.R., 2003. Catastrophic regime shifts in ecosystems: linking theory to observation. *Trends in Ecology and Evolution,* vol. 18: 648–56.

Schepman, T., 2015. Tomates sans eau ni pesticide : cette méthode fascine les biologistes, *L'Obs Rue 89,* March 4 [online] Available at: <http://rue89.nouvelobs.com/2015/03/09/tomates-sans-eau-ni-pesticide-cette-methode-fascine-les-biologistes-257958>

Schmidt, M.J., 2013. Amazonian dark earths: pathways to sustainable development in tropical rainforests?. *Bol. Mus. Para. Emílio Goeldi. Cienc. Hum.*, Belém, vol. 8 no. 1: 11–38. [online] Available at: <http://www.scielo.br/pdf/bgoeldi/v8n1/v8n1a02.pdf> [Accessed 14.7.15]

Schramski, J.R., Gattie, D.K. and Brown, J.H., 2015. Human domination of the biosphere: rapid discharge of the earth-space battery foretells the future of humankind. *Proceedings of the National Academy of Sciences*, vol. 112 no. 31: 9511–17.

Schubert, C., 2013. How to evaluate creative destruction: reconstructing Schumpeter's approach. *Cambridge Journal of Economics*, vol. 37 no. 2. DOI: 10.1093/cje/bes055, published online: 22 January.

Schumpeter, J., 1976 [1943]. *Capitalism, socialism and democracy*. 5th edition. London: George Allen & Unwin.

Science China Press, 2015. Organic farming can reverse the agriculture ecosystem from a carbon source to a carbon sink. Press release 29 April. [online] Available at: <http://www.eurekalert.org/pub_releases/2015-04/scp-ofc042915.php> [Accessed 4.9.15]

Science News, 2015. *Chemists devise technology that could transform solar energy storage*, 19 June. [online] Available at: <http://www.sciencedaily.com/releases/2015/06/150619103601.htm> [Accessed 1.8.16]

SEER Centre, n.d. About SEER. [online] Available at: <http://www.seercentre.org.uk/about-us/> [Accessed 1.8.16]

Self-Help Housing, n.d. [online] Available at: <http://self-help-housing.org/case-studies/bonnington-square-london/> [Accessed 4.10.12].

Service, T., 2013. A guide to Yannis Xenakis' music. Guardian, blog post, 23 April. [online] Available at: <http://www.theguardian.com/music/tomserviceblog/2013/apr/23/contemporary-music-guide-xenakis> [Accessed 3.12.13]

Seufferheld, M.J., 2015. Interview in *Science Daily*, 9 June. [online] Available at: <http://www.sciencedaily.com/releases/2015/06/150609113909.htm> [Accessed 1.8.16]

Shames, C., 1981. The scientific humanism of Lucien Sève. *Science & Society*, vol. 45 no. 1 (Spring): 1–23.

Shapira, M., 2016. Gut microbiotas and host evolution: scaling up symbiosis. *Trends in Ecology and Evolution*, vol. 31 no. 7 DOI: 10.1016/j.tree.2016.03.006

Shedlock, M., 2016. World's first robot-run lettuce farm to produce 30,000 heads daily; tipping point for workerless agriculture, blog post, 28 January. [online] Available at: <http://globaleconomicanalysis.blogspot.co.uk/2016/01/worlds-first-robot-run-lettuce-farm-to.html> [Accessed 4.3.16]

Shen, M. et al., 2015. Evaporative cooling over the Tibetan Plateau induced by vegetation growth. *Proceedings of the National Academy of Sciences*, vol. 112 no. 30: 9299.

Shiva, V., 1988. *Staying alive – women, ecology and development*. London: Zed Books.

Shuffield, R., 2006. *Thomas Sankara: the upright man*, feature film. [online] Available at: <https://www.youtube.com/watch?v=xgD-jhBIdiQ> [Accessed 1.8.16]

Slater, T., 2014. *The resilience of neoliberal urbanism*. Open Democracy posting, 28 January. [online] Available at: <https://www.opendemocracy.net/opensecurity/tom-slater/resilience-of-neoliberal-urbanism> [Accessed 15.5.15]

Slow Food International, 2016. Indigenous voices. [online] Available at: <http://www.slowfood.com/what-we-do/themes/indigenous/indigenous-voices/> [Accessed 1.8.16]

Smith, M.E., 1996. The Aztec silent majority. In A. G. Mastache de Escobar (ed.) *Arquaeologia Mesoamericana: homenaje a William T. Sanders*, vol. 1. pp. 375–86.

Smolin, L., 2013. *Time reborn*. London: Allen Lane.

Soil Association, n.d. Frequently asked questions. [online] Available at: <http://www.soilassociation.org/frequentlyaskedquestions/smid/4313?key=conversion+period> [Accessed 11.1.16]

Solon, O., 2015. Bees put to work lugging pesticides to flowers. *New Scientist* No. 3045, 31 October: 13.

Song, X. et al., 2014. Chinese Grain for Green program led to highly increased soil organic carbon levels: a meta-analysis. *Nature - Scientific Reports*, vol. 4, article number 4460 DOI:10.1038/srep04460. [online] Available at: <http://www.nature.com/articles/srep04460> [Accessed 1.8.16]

Song, Y. et al., 2010. Interplant communication of tomato plants through underground common mycorrhizal networks. *PLoS ONE*, vol. 5 no.: e13324, 13 October.

Steiner, C., 2009. Biochar carbon sequestration. In: T. Goreau, ed. *Green ThinDisc, an interactive multimedia book*. United Nations Commission on Sustainable Develoment Partnership in New Technologies for Small Island Developing States, prepared for COP15. Chapter 17.

Strogatz, S., 2003. *Sync: the emerging science of spontaneous order*. London: Penguin.

Stuart, K., 2015. Climate Hope City: how Minecraft can tell the story of climate change. *The Guardian*, blog post, 12 June [online] Available at: <http://www.theguardian.com/environment/keep-it-in-the-ground-blog/2015/jun/12/climate-hope-city-how-minecraft-can-tell-the-story-of-climate-change?CMP=share_btn_fb> [Accessed 1.8.16]

Suliman, M., 1999. Conflict resolution among the Borana and the Fur – similar features, different outcomes. In: M. Suliman, ed. *Ecology, politics and violent conflict*. 1999. London: Zed.

Sustain, 2014. *Reaping rewards: can communities grow a million meals for London?* [online] Available at: <http://www.sustainweb.org/publications/?id=306&dm_i=8UC,2PW-4G,13QXAD,9X0AZ,1> [Accessed 4.10.15]

Tao, L. et al., 2015. Disease ecology across soil boundaries: effects of below-ground fungi on above-ground host–parasite interactions. *Proceedings of the Royal Society B*, vol. 282 no. 1817, October DOI: 10.1098/rspb.2015.1993

Taussig, M.T., 1980. *The devil and commodity fetishism in South America*. Chapel Hill: University of North Carolina Press.

Taylor, L.L. et al., 2015. Enhanced weathering strategies for stabilizing climate and averting ocean acidification. *Nature Climate Change*. DOI: 10.1038/nclimate2882

Tebaldi, C. et al., 2006. Going to the extremes – an intercomparison of model-simulated historical and future changes in extreme events. *Climatic Change*, vol. 79: 185–211.

Tegmark, M., 2014. Solid. Liquid. Consciousness. *New Scientist*, 12 April: 28

Terre et Humanisme, 2014. *Sur le terrain: Burkina Faso*. [online] Available at: <http://terre-humanisme.org/sur-le-terrain/burkina-faso> [Accessed 30.1.15]

The Week, 2012 *Americans' ton-a-year eating habit: By the numbers*. [online] Available at: <http://theweek.com/articles/479150/americans-tonayear-eating-habit-by-numbers> [Accessed 1.8.16]

Thelen, E., 1989. Self-organisation in developmental processes – can systems approaches work? In: M.R. Gunnar and E. Thelen, eds. *Systems and development: the Minnesota symposia on child psychology*, volume 22. New York: Psychology Press.

Thirsk, J., 1997. *Alternative agriculture, a history: from the black death to the present day*. Oxford: Oxford University Press.

Thompson, E., 1980. Notes on exterminism, the last stage of civilization. *New Left Review*, vol. I no. 121, May–June.

Thorner, D., 1971. Peasant economy as a category in economic history. In: T. Shanin ed. *Peasants and peasant societies*. London: Penguin.

Tian, H. et al., 2016. The terrestrial biosphere as a net source of greenhouse gases to the atmosphere. *Nature*, vol. 531 no. 7593: 225 DOI: 10.1038/nature16946

Tiberius, V., 2011. Path dependence, path breaking, and path creation: a theoretical scaffolding for futures studies? *Journal of Futures Studies*, vol. 15 no. 4, June.

Tierney, K., 2002. Strength of a city: a disaster research perspective on the world trade center attack. *10 Years after September 11* (a Social Science Research Council Essay Forum). [online] Available at: <http://essays.ssrc.org/10yearsafter911/strength-of-a-city-a-disaster-research-perspective-on-the-world-trade-center-attack/> [Accessed 7.8.16]

Tomasello, M. et al., 2005. Understanding and sharing intentions: The origins of cultural cognition. *Behavioral And Brain Sciences*, vol. 28.

Tomkins, M., 2014. *Making space for food: everyday community food gardening and its contribution to urban agriculture*, PhD, University of Brighton. [online] Available at: <http://eprints.brighton.ac.uk/12919/1/Mikey%20Tomkins.pdf> [Accessed 1.8.16]

Tornaghi, C. and Van Dyck, B., 2014. Research-informed gardening activism: steering the public food and land agenda. *Local Environment*, (ahead-of-print): 1–18.

Tulowiecki, S.J. and Larsen, C.S., 2015. Native American impacts on past forest composition inferred from species distribution models, Chautauqua County, NY. *Ecological Monographs*, 150519114917002 DOI: 10.1890/14-2259.1

UCL (University College London), 2015. *Symposium: climate change: adaptation, resilience and risk*, 2 June.

UK Government, 1998. *Select Committee on Environment, Transport and Regional Affairs fifth report; appendix II: modern allotments legislation*. [online] Available at: <http://www.publications.parliament.uk/pa/cm199798/cmselect/cmenvtra/560/56002.htm> [Accessed 1.8.16]

UK Government, 2011. *Foresight. The future of food and farming: challenges and choices for global sustainability final project report*. London: The Government Office for Science.

UNCTAD [United Nations Conference on Trade and Development], 2013. *Trade and environment review: make agriculture truly sustainable now for food security in a changing climate*. Geneva, UNCTAD/DIC/TED/2012/3. Available at: http://unctad.org/en/PublicationsLibrary/ditcted2012d3_en.pdf . [Accessed 1.8.16]

Uncube magazine, 2014. *The urban commons*. 3 April. [online] Available at: <http://www.uncubemagazine.com/magazine-20-12467995.html#!/page1> [Accessed 11.2.15]

University of California – San Diego, 2015. New era in robotics: 3-D-printed robot is hard at heart, soft on the outside: first of its kind robot is inspired by nature, capable of multiple jumps. *ScienceDaily*, 9 July.

University of Iowa, 2015. Local food movement rooted in relationships and values. *ScienceDaily*, 22 August.

University of Michigan, 2016. More ancient viruses lurk in our DNA than we thought. *ScienceDaily*, 22 March.

University of Wageningen, 2014. *Terra preta do Indio: Recovering the past, regaining the future of Amazonian dark earths*, research project [online] Available at: <https://www.wageningenur.nl/en/show/terra-preta-do-indio.htm> [Accessed 1.8.16]

University of Washington, 2015. Plants make big decisions with microscopic cellular competition. *ScienceDaily*, 18 June. [online] Available at: <www.sciencedaily.com/releases/2015/06/150618104159.htm> [Accessed 1.3.16]

University of Wisconsin-Madison, 2015. Mycologist says our close relatives break the bounds of biology. *ScienceDaily*, 26 October. [online] Available at: <www.sciencedaily.com/releases/2015/10/151026181713.htm> [Accessed 6.11.15]

Urban Gardening Manifest, 2014. *Die Stadt ist Unser Garten*. [online] Available at: <http://urbangardeningmanifest.de/> [Accessed 1.8.16]

Vaidya, N. et al., 2012. Spontaneous network formation among cooperative RNA replicators. *Nature*, vol. 491(7422), 1 November 72–7. DOI: 10.1038/nature11549. Epub 2012 Oct 17.

van der Heijden, M.G. et al., 2008. The unseen majority: soil microbes as drivers of plant diversity and productivity in terrestrial ecosystems. *Ecology Letters*, vol. 11: 296–310 DOI: 10.1111/j.1461-0248.2007.01139.x

van der Velden, N., 2015. *Biodiversity, productivity and scale in resilient food production systems*, presentation, International Permaculture Conference 2015, London, 9 September.

van Groeningen, K.J. et al., 2014. Faster decomposition under increased atmospheric CO2 limits soil carbon storage. *Science*, vol. 344 no. 6183 DOI: 10.1126/science.1249534

van Meter, K. et al., 2016. The nitrogen legacy: emerging evidence of nitrogen accumulation in anthropogenic landscapes. *Environmental Research Letters*, vol. 11 no: 035014 DOI: 10.1088/1748-9326/11/3/035014

Vassallo, C. et al., 2015. Cell rejuvenation and social behaviors promoted by LPS exchange in myxobacteria. *Proceedings of the National Academy of Sciences*; 201503553 DOI: 10.1073/pnas.1503553112

Vattel, E. de., 1972 [1758]. *The law of nations*, reprinted in P.D. Curtin ed., *Imperialism*. London: Macmillan.

Vila-Viñas, D. and Barandiaran, X., 2015. The FLOK doctrine. *The Journal of Peer Production*, no. (July).

von Liebig, J., 1844. *Familiar letters on chemistry*, Letter XI. [online] Available at: <https://ia902604.us.archive.org/29/items/familiarletterso04524gut/chmlt10.txt> [Accessed 1.8.16]

von Tunzelmann, N., 2003. Historical coevolution of governance and technology in the industrial revolutions. *Structural Change and Economic Dynamics*, vol. 14: 365–84.

Walker, J., *Obituary of Colin Ward*. [online] Available at: <http://reason.com/blog/2010/02/17/colin-ward-rip Accessed October 2011> [Accessed 18.11.11]

Wall, D., 2015. Interview in *Science Daily*, 21 May. [online] Available at: <http://www.sciencedaily.com/releases/2015/05/150521133738.htm> [Accessed 1.8.16]

Wallace, R., 2015. *Is consciousness inherently unstable? An iterated Data Rate Theorem model of high metabolic demand in neural tissues*, 19 July. [online] Available at: <https://peerj.com/preprints/1236.pdf> [Accessed 15.11.15]

Wan, P.Y., 2013. Dialectics, complexity, and the systemic approach toward a critical reconciliation. *Philosophy of the Social Sciences*. vol. 43 no.4 (December): 411–52.

Wang, Y. et al., 2011. Long-term impact of farming practices on soil organic carbon and nitrogen pools and microbial biomass and activity. *Soil and Tillage Research*, vol. 117: 8–16.

Ward, C., 1973. *Anarchy in action*. London: George Allen and Unwin.

Weitling, W., 1979 [1838]. L'humanité telle qu'elle est et telle qu'elle devrait être. In: G.M. Bravo, ed. *Les Socialistes avant Marx*, Tome II. Paris: Maspero.

Welch, R.M. and Graham, R.D., 1999. A new paradigm for world agriculture meeting human needs: productive, sustainable, nutritious. *Field Crops Research*, vol. 60: 1–10.

Wharton, C., 2016. Food hubs – A new opportunity for local food systems. In: R. Phillips and C. Wharton, eds. *Local food systems and community development*. Abingdon: Routledge.

Whitefield, P., 2004. *The Earth care manual: a permaculture handbook for Britain and other temperate climates*. East Meon, Hampshire: Permanent Publications.

Willes, M., 2014. *The gardens of the British working class*. New Haven CT: Yale University Press.

Williams, W.L., 1992. *The spirit and the flesh: sexual diversity in American Indian culture*. Boston MA: Beacon Press.

Wilson, A., 2009. Growing food locally: integrating agriculture into the built environment. *Environmental Building News*, vol. 18 no 2.

Winn, S., 2009. A paradise built in hell – the extraordinary communities that arise in disaster by Rebecca Solnit (book review), *San Francisco Chronicle*, 23 August.

Winstanley, G. et al., 1983 [1649]. The true Levellers' standard advanced: or, the state of community opened, and presented to the sons of men. In: G. Winstanley, *The Law of Freedom and other Writings* (ed. Christopher Hill). Cambridge: Cambridge University Press.

Wiskerke, J.C., 2015. Urban food systems. In: H. de Zeeuw and P. Drechsel, eds. *Cities and agriculture – developing resilient urban food systems*. London: Earthscan.

World People's Conference on Climate Change and the Rights of Mother Earth, 2010. *People's agreement of cochabamba*. 20 April. [online] Available at: <http://pwccc.wordpress.com/2010/04/24/peoples-agreement/> [Accessed 1.8.16]

Wright, E.O., 2010. *Envisioning real utopias*. London: Verso.

Wright, J., 2012. The little-studied success story of post-crisis food security in Cuba: does lack of international interest signify lack of political will? *International Journal of Cuban Studies*, vol. 4 no. 2: 130–53.

Xenakis, I., 1955. *Metastasis*: orchestral composition. [online] Available at: <http://www.youtube.com/watch?v=SZazYFchLRI> [Accessed 1.10.15]

Yau, S.-T., 2010. *The shape of inner space – string theory and the geometry of the universe's hidden dimensions*. New York: Basic Books.

Zelem, M.C., 1991. L'evolution des techniques fromagères dans le Cantal, France du XVIII au XIX Siècle. In: G. Dupré ed. *Savoirs paysans et développement*. Paris: Karthala/Orstom.

Zhang, W.-F. et al., 2013. New technologies reduce greenhouse gas emissions from nitrogenous fertilizer in China. *Proceedings of the National Academy of Sciences*, vol. 110 no. 21 (May): 8375–80. Published online 13 May 2013. DOI: 10.1073/pnas.1210447110

Zhu, Z. et al., 2016. Greening of the Earth and its drivers. *Nature Climate Change*. DOI: 10.1038/nclimate3004

Zimet, A., 2012. *Guerrilla grafters: undoing civilization one fruitless branch at a time*. [online] Available at: <http://www.commondreams.org/further/2012/04/10-0> [Accessed 14.6.12]

Ziska, L. et al., 2016: Food safety, nutrition, and distribution. In U.S. Global Change Research Program, *The impacts of climate change on human health in the United States: a scientific assessment*. Washington DC. pp. 189–216. [online] Available at: <http://dx.doi.org/10.7930/J0ZP4417> [Accessed 1.8.16]

Zocco, M., 2015. Ron Finley's latest South LA garden grows renewed community interest in fresh foods. *Intersections South LA*, 20 July. [online] Available at: <http://intersectionssouthla.org/story/ron-finleys-latest-south-la-garden-grows-renewed-community-interest-in-fresh-foods/> [Accessed 4.12.15]

Zwick, M., 1983. *Incompleteness, negation, hazard: on the precariousness of systems*. Discussion paper. Portland OR: Portland State University.

Index

agribusiness (corporate interests) 14–15, 95, 115, 118, 120–1
  see also imperialism
agroecology 4, 27, 36, 49, 53, 70, 80, 87, 96, 99, 109, 122–3
agroforestry 53, 61–2, 93
alienation 12–13, 23, 89, 110, 124
Allen, Will 107
allotments 1, 27, 51, 93
Amin, Samir 78

Baran, Paul 78
Bateson, Gregory 45
Biko, Steve 87
Blake, William 123
biomimicry 73–4, 90, 93, 96

Caldwell, Malcolm 16, 79, 100
capitalism 66, 78, 86, 106
  accumulation circuits 7, 10, 46
  capitalist mode of production, historical phases of 12, 14–15, 24, 27, 75, 82, 87–8
  'entropy' of 84
chaos
  chaotic behaviour of systems 28–9, 59, 113
  creative facet of 22, 43, 45–6, 55, 93, 105, 111
  manipulative notions of, in ruling discourse 48–9, 113
Chartists 109
Chayanov, A.V. 88
chemical-based farming 2, 6, 8–9, 15–16, 23, 53, 64, 75–6, 79, 87
class, social
  centrality of class struggle in social analysis 10, 12–15, 26, 35, 37, 44–5, 54, 97, 111–2
  in understanding food insecurity 27, 98
  working-class tradition 1–3, 102, 114
  in pre-capitalist society 52–3, 89
  and national liberation 54–5
climate (state/regime shift) 21 *see also* earth system
  mitigation/adaptation 22, 66–73, 101
colonialism ('modernisation') 11, 13, 40, 48–9, 54, 58, 77–8, 89, 104, 106–7
commons regimes 3, 37, 54–5, 66, 72, 86, 89, 97, 102, 108, 119–22
  enclosure of 12, 16
  'tragedy of' 36

complexity 3, 20, 45, 53, 64, 70, 89, 91–2, 118
  in soil and ecology 17, 30–4, 80, 105
  in society 114, 120
  see also self-organisation
compost 100–2
Community Supported Agriculture 10, 88–9, 98–9
consciousness (conscientisation) 44–6
co-operation 34–9, 102, 110, 119
co-optation 96, 107, 109–12, 121
Corbusier, Le 103
corporate interests *see* agribusiness
crisis 24–8
Cuba 117–8

Darwin, Charles 31, 35–6
Dawkins, Richard 36
Dependency theory 78, 83, 86
de Schutter, Olivier 4
desertification 17
design and planning 42, 45, 90, 96, 103, 105, 123
dialectics 40–5, 50, 55, 59, 69, 74, 96, 112, 117–8, 123
distributive justice 6

earth system (Gaia) 21, 31, 66–9
Eisenstein, Sergei 103
energy (work) 3, 8, 50–1, 53, 67, 70, 79–80, 85–6, 111
Engels, Frederick 14, 41, 43–4, 46
entropy 3, 15–16, 18–19, 31, 42, 48, 51–2, 64, 70, 79, 92
environment
  environmental justice 1, 3, 20, 110, 113
  environmentalist movements 14, 71–2, 85
  and 'rift' in development 20, 23, 56–7, 65, 73, 91
  built 33, 90, 94, 105
  role in evolution 33, 35, 37, 56, 60,
  and ecosystem services 34, 58
  in plant breeding 62–3
  in the definition of life 69, 73
  see also 'wildness'
equilibrium 18–20, 55, 58–9, 69–70, 73, 91–2, 96, 105, 108, 110
evolution 20, 22, 30–1, 35–8, 40, 43, 59–65, 90–1, 93, 105, 116, 119

143

Fanon, Frantz 87, 106
farms/farmers
  small 4–5, 84–9
  livelihoods of 51, 81, 99–100
  origins of 61–2
  labour-intensiveness 53, 85
  subordination to accumulation 7, 10, 12, 14–16, 26, 76, 78, 80, 84, 87–8
  conversion to organics 9, 115, 117
  farmer experimentation 16, 19, 49, 54, 62–4, 72, 77, 97
  farmer suicides in India 7, 116
  in experimental archaeology 53
  and environment 58, 60
  urban and peri-urban 71, 89, 93, 98–101
  vertical 96
  role in societal transition 119, 123
fascism/Nazism 110–1
feedback (in regulation of systems) 8, 10, 20, 46, 67–70, 92
feminist critique 11, 16, 43, 56, 76–7, 86, 104
  see also 'mastering' nature
food-price spikes 10, 14
food security 4, 22, 81–2, 93, 112
  see also risk
food sovereignty 50, 54–5, 88–9, 122, 124
  definition 7–8, 114
  intrinsic link with agroecology 36, 87, 109,
  and conscientisation 44,
  and critique of neo-colonialism 77–8
Forbes, Jack D. 80
force 9
Foucault, Michel 9, 24, 56, 87, 112, 123
Freire, Paulo 44, 87, 123
Fukuoka, Masanobu 49, 51–2, 91, 113, 123
Fuller, Buckminster 123

general systems theory 40, 110–3
genetic modification 12, 63, 75–6
gentrification 106, 112
Goodwin, Brian 45
Gramsci, Antonio 9, 24
Green Revolution 5, 12, 23, 43–4, 75–6, 116–7
green roofs 95
gathering 59, 61
Gaudí, Antoni 104
'guerrilla' (gardening, urbanism) 113

Hegel, G.F.W. 40–2, 113
Hobbes, Thomas 13, 35–6, 39, 111
Holling, C.S. 20, 28, 98, 103, 111
Hopkins, Rob 111
Howard, Alfred 17, 49
Howard, Ebenezer 104
Hundertwasser, Friedensreich 104

Ilenkov, E.V. 46, 117
imperialism 43, 74–9, 81–2, 84, 88–9, 117
indigenous (traditional) thought 36, 39, 55–6, 59, 61, 71, 73, 94, 102
  readiness to embrace disturbance 22, 57, 96
  and the negation of the negation 40, 42–3, 121
  duality within tradition 50, 52–3, 54, 78, 86, 107, 110

as inspiration for today's sustainability movements 49–50, 80, 96, 118,
  'deep tradition' as distinct from elite rule 52
  see also Native American farming systems
indoor growing (aquaponics) 97
intercropping see agroforestry

Jacobs, Jane 105
Jones, Mark 77

knowledge 3, 16, 54
Kluge, Alexander 103
Krasil'nikov, N.A. 117
Kropotkin, Peter 108, 114

land grabs 11, 16
land rights
  see radical social movements
Lenin, V.I. 41, 44, 46, 74–5, 115, 117, 120, 122
livelihoods 23, 98, 109
livestock 71
Luxemburg, Rosa 84
Lysenko, T.D. 115

Malthus, Thomas (and Malthusianism) 3, 13–14, 20, 35–7, 39, 79, 100, 102, 110
Mao Zedong 78
margins (edges) 46, 49, 55–7, 59, 73 see also permaculture
Marx, Karl (and Marxism) 14–15, 19, 108, 115, 118, 122
  confluence with organics 2, 17, 40–1, 46–7, 53, 103
  and cost of subsistence 6, 84
  and the role of land in capitalist relations 15
  and development of systems 24, 43–4, 113
  'mastering' nature 11–12, 48, 114, 119
  see also feminist critique
Merchant, Carolyn 43, 48, 76
metabolism 19, 106–7
modernism 42, 48, 59, 103–7, 111–2
Morin, Edgar 112–3

Native American farming systems 22, 49, 54, 57, 59, 62, 72, 80, 94, 96, 115
  see also indigenous (traditional) thought
Naxalite revolutionary movement (India) 78
neo-liberalism 14, 27, 35, 45, 54, 81–4, 88, 106–7, 111–2
networks 3, 98, 102, 118–9, 123
nitrogen pollution 6, 17, 100
Noble, Dennis 37
no-till farming 51
Nowak, Martin 37

organic food and agriculture 16–17, 36, 42, 49, 51, 113
  conversion from chemical-based farming 9, 33, 117–8
  in relation to general systems theory 2, 46–7
  rapprochement with radical politics 40, 53
  and carbon sequestration 70–1
  possible co-optation by ruling discourses 109
Ostrom, Elinor 121

panarchy 22, 55, 105, 113–4
'paradigm shift' 1, 4–5, 8, 10, 13–14, 27, 30, 33–4, 40, 42, 44, 55–8, 66, 74, 85, 87–8, 90–1, 96, 98
path-dependency 8–9
peasant resistance and land-rights movements 13, 108–9, 122, 124
permaculture 45, 49–50, 53, 55, 111, 118, 123
Physiocrat school of economics 16, 102
Polanyi, Karl 88
Polanyi, Michael 88
Political Ecology 8, 24, 34, 103, 106
pre-Socratic philosophers 20, 40–1, 42–3, 113
Prigogine, Ilya 36, 40, 104
'prisoners' dilemma' 37
Purple, Adam 105

Rabhi, Pierre 80, 113
radical social movements 15, 27, 42, 50, 53–4, 74, 80, 88, 99, 102, 106–8, 110, 112, 120, 124
reductionism (homogenisation), critique of 5, 12, 16–18, 22–3, 27, 33, 35–6, 40–3, 59–60, 63, 76, 81–2, 83, 87, 91, 98, 118, 120
resilience 23, 60, 63–5, 92, 96, 99, 105, 112
 see also climate mitigation/adaptation
Reynolds, P.J. 53, 59–60
Ricardo, David 80
Richards, Paul 49
risk 2–3, 65, 97–9
Rostow, Walt W. 77–8

Sankara, Thomas 80
Schumpeter, Joseph 24
seeds 12, 63–4, 75–6, 89, 120
self-organisation 8, 10, 20, 22, 30–1, 35, 52, 55–6, 63, 72, 87, 90–1, 93, 96, 104–5, 111, 113–14, 123
socialism 115–7

soil systems 17, 19, 31–3, 52, 69–70
solar energy 95
Stalin J.V. 116
Steiner, Rudolf 111
'sustainable intensification' 4, 34, 100, 102

terra preta (dark earth, biochar) 72–3
Thompson, E.P. 77
transition
 definition 8
 gradualism and radicalism in 9, 13, 40, 43,
 and conversion to organics 10
 to low-carbon society 29, 66,
 and 'criticality' in systems theory 46,
 and historical phase shift 57, 123
 and socialism 115, 118
Transition Towns movement 111, 118

UN Food and Agriculture Organisation (FAO) 1, 4, 7, 27, 71, 76, 85–6
urbanisation 13, 16, 85
urban systems (metabolism) 90–1, 93–6, 101, 105
USSR/Russia 115–7

Vavilov, N.I. 115–6
visioning futures 18, 35, 39, 44–5, 57, 66, 89, 93, 104, 106, 108, 121–3
von Bertalanffy, Ludwig 110
von Hayek, Friedrich 106
von Liebig, Justus 17, 19

waste (food) 5
Ward, Colin 114, 120, 122
Weitling, Wilhelm 108
Winstanley, Gerrard 122–4
'wildness' 34, 48, 50, 56, 58–60, 93–4

Xenakis, Iannis 103

Zapatistas 122–4
Ziegler, Jean 4